Exploring Fort Worth with Children

Michael S. Bumagin, M.D.

Republic of Texas Press

Library of Congress Cataloging-in-Publication Data

Bumagin, Michael S.
  Exploring Fort Worth with children / Michael S. Bumagin.
      p.   cm.
  Includes index.
  ISBN 1-55622-734-5
  1. Fort Worth (Tex.)–Guidebooks.   2. Family recreation–Texas–
Fort Worth–Guidebooks.   3. Children–Travel–Texas–Fort Worth–Guidebooks.
  I. Title.
  F394.F7 B85   2000   00-025489
  917.64'53150464—dc21   CIP

ISBN 1-55622-734-5
10 9 8 7 6 5 4 3 2 1
0002

All inquiries for volume purchases of this book should be addressed to
Wordware Publishing, Inc., at 2320 Los Rios Boulevard, Plano, Texas
75074. Telephone inquiries may be made by calling:

(972) 423-0090

Contents

Contents

Contents

Contents

Contents

Contents

Contents

Chapter 19
When Something Unexpected Happens 201

Chapter 20
Miscellaneous 211

Contents

Contents

Acknowledgements

At times it seemed like this project would *never* be done. Indeed, it might not have come to fruition without the help and encouragement of many people.

The author line, by rights, should have the names of all the members of The Writers Group of Fort Worth. Without their astute critique, who knows how many more goofs, gaffes and literary blunders might have slipped in? The errors, if any, are mine; the clear, smooth, concise writing is due to their helpful recommendations. Special thanks are due Robyn Weaver, who runs the Group and keeps it from becoming too rowdy. Her thoughtful commentary has made the narrative flow.

Thanks also to Writers Group members: Ann Arnold, Linda Austin, Frank Ball, Dianne McCartney, Jeffrey McClanahan, Rhonda Samudio, Kathy Foster, Mike Vick, David Walker and too many others to list here. Without their sharp eyes, ears, and pencils much of what you're reading would not have been as readable.

Thanks to Lucile Davis for "all the bubbles."

Ginnie Bivona, my editor from Wordware's Republic of Texas Press, kept me on track with regular "Where's my book?" phone calls. Without her, the manuscript might still be languishing unfinished in one of the stacks on my desk.

Last, but never least, heartfelt love and appreciation to My Wife Myra, who has tolerated those stacks all around the house and kept me from despairing of ever getting done. She has maintained the rest of our life and balanced the checkbook, too. Here's hoping the royalties will make that chore more difficult!

Introduction

Foat Wuth Ah Luv Yew!

Where the west begins is a big city with a hometown heart. Fort Worth, Texas, the western half of the D/FW Metroplex, has all the amenities of her sister to the east. Coupled with a slower-paced existence, it makes our city a nice place to raise a family *and* a great place to visit. The "West-O-Plex," in addition to metropolitan Fort Worth, includes numerous surrounding subdivisions, ranging in size from country village (like Keller, Coppell, and Southlake) to such small cities as Arlington, home of the Texas Rangers baseball team, and Irving, headquarters of the Dallas Cowboys.

While each residential area has its own flavor and personality, all are part of the whole, and a friendly "Howdy, Neighbor" attitude pervades. Fort Worth residents (and even police officers) are likely to *show* a lost traveler where they want to go instead of merely giving directions. This attitude is contagious, and it results in a relaxed lifestyle that tells the visitor to take time to smell the flowers.

And Fort Worth has plenty of flowers, from the profusion of April's bursting bluebonnets (the state flower) to the riot of color flooding roadsides and pastures all summer. Much of the credit for this goes to the tireless work of former "First Ladybird" Johnson and her National Wildflower Center in Austin.

Named for a military man who never set foot in the city that would eventually bear his name, Fort Worth was founded in 1849 as one of several outposts established to guard the Texas frontier from the potential menace of the Indian. It achieved prominence as a commercial center with the development of the beef industry and the arrival of the railroads connecting to the West Coast and the Rocky Mountains via the Texas and Pacific and, later, the Fort Worth and Denver Railways.

Fort Worth is a family town in more ways than one. A particular family (Bass) plays a dominant role in the city's economic development. With a share in the ownership of several of the major structures in downtown Fort Worth (including the City Center Towers, The Worthington Hotel, and the Caravan of Dreams), they have a vested interest in the prosperity and quality of life of Fort Worth. The recent completion of the Bass Performance Hall places this city on equal footing with Dallas and, perhaps, New York as a site for the finest in concert and theatrical performing arts.

Visitors from all parts of the world and of all ages can find something here to interest and excite them. Let's take a look at some of the fun things to see and do in COWTOWN, USA. Fort Worth, Texas, is waiting to make you feel at home!

Chapter 1

Uniquely Fort Worth

Some sights bring certain things to mind. We see the Eiffel Tower and think of Paris (the one in France, not the one in north Texas). The Gateway Arch reminds us of St. Louis, Missouri. And the Golden Gate Bridge tells us we're in San Francisco.

Now, thanks to the magic of television, a Fort Worth landmark has millions of Americans thinking of—can you beat this?—*Dallas*! When *Walker, Texas Ranger* began filming in Fort Worth, it disrupted downtown traffic for days. Every Saturday night, the "Dallas" office of the Texas Rangers is shown and all America sees the Fort Worth Courthouse. That's the price Fort Worth pays for not shooting J. R. Ewing.

However, Fort Worth does have some special landmarks all its own:

The Stockyards

On Fort Worth's north side, this national historic district celebrates the early days of the cattle industry when the name Cowtown really meant COW town. The area contains numerous shops, restaurants, saloons, and hotels decorated in period style. The Visitors Center at 130 Exchange Avenue (817-624-4741) can get your tour off to a great start. Across the street, in the Livestock Exchange Building, you will find

1

Texas Longhorns in front of "Cowtown" Mural. Photo courtesy of J. Reagan Ferguson

the Stockyards Museum and the North Fort Worth Historical Society.

Billy Bob's Texas—the world's largest honky-tonk—occupies a prominent place in the center of the district (2520 Rodeo Plaza/817-624-7117) and features frequently sold-out performances by country and western stars.

The Stockyards Station used to be the hog and sheep pens but now serves as a terminus for the Tarantula Railroad, which makes a pleasant day-excursion as far as Grapevine, TX.

Water Gardens

Another part of Fort Worth immortalized in film, this 4.3-acre park with sculpture and fountains made a brief appearance in the science fiction motion picture *Logan's Run*. Located in the East End of downtown, it is open seven days a week from 10 A.M. to 10 P.M. free of charge. The kids can even play in the fountains. No fishing, please; there are no fish. It's a grand place to stroll or simply sit and commune with nature. Take a picnic lunch, find a shady spot, and unwind.

1502 Commerce Street
at Houston Street

817-871-7698

Stock Show

One of many horse and cattle exhibits held throughout the year, the Southwestern Exposition and Livestock Show & Rodeo runs for two to three weeks each year at the end of January and the beginning of February. With the flavor of a county fair, it has something for children of all ages.

Will Rogers Memorial Center   817-877-2400
3301 West Lancaster Avenue   www.fwssr.com
Fort Worth, Texas 76107

Casa Manana

Not far from the Will Rogers Complex, Casa is a theatre in the round covered by a geodesic dome. Its curving silver foil profile is a Fort Worth signature, and it has seating for more than 1800 people. Each year the theatre group performs children's plays, a summer musical season, and a winter season of plays and concerts. A theatre school begins the training of the next generation of dramatic artists. In addition, it provides a venue for visiting acts. Even Jerry Seinfeld has graced its stage.

3101 West Lancaster Avenue   817-332-2272
www.ssi-mis.com/casamanana

Bass Performance Hall

This recently completed (1998) architectural masterpiece brings world-class acoustical magnificence to downtown Fort Worth with a facility second to none. The home of the Fort Worth Symphony Orchestra and the Fort Worth Opera, it will also host visiting performers and musical theatre. It premiered with *Phantom of The Opera*. The quality of sound transmission is so spectacular that there are NO BAD SEATS in the house.

Its exterior features striking, high relief angels holding great golden trumpets over the heads of passers-by. Inside, high vaulted ceilings rise above the gleaming marble foyer and curving stairways. The painted central dome gives the illusion that the roof is open to a blue, cloud-filled sky.

330 East Fourth Street
Fourth and Calhoun Streets
Fort Worth, Texas 76102

817-212-4200
Tickets: 817-212-4280
1-888-597-STAR (7827)

Sundance Square

In the middle of downtown, surrounded by banks, eateries, office buildings, and parking lots, there's a huge mural depicting longhorns that have come to symbolize Texas as they started up the Chisholm Trail. The artist, Richard Haas, covered three sides of the 1907 Jett Building to remind us of the cattle drives of the 1860s and 70s. Come see it!

Caravan of Dreams

Fort Worth's other dome on the roof of a building in the middle of downtown covers a center that features top- name performers year round. From the rooftop garden you can relax with beverages and snacks in an open-air setting over-looking Sundance Square.

312 Houston Street   817-877-3000
Fort Worth, Texas   www.caravanofdreams.com

Tarantula Train

Rent the whole train or a single car for a special occasion. Or, buy single tickets to tour from the Stockyards all the way to Grapevine in the northeast part of the county. The kids will love the open-air ride in the country, and either end of the route offers plenty of activities.

140 E. Exchange Avenue   **Cottonbelt Depot**
Fort Worth, Texas 76106   507 S. Main Street
Tickets: 817-625-7245   Grapevine, Texas
FAX: 817-738-9657   Metro Reservations:
1-800-952-5717   817-654-0898
www.tarantula.com

Chapter 2

Historic Landmarks

In the one hundred and fifty years since its founding, Fort Worth has seen a wealth of intriguing history. Remembrances of the flow of time are all around. From the first days of the Stockyards, through the coming of the railroads and the automobile, all the way up to President John Fitzgerald Kennedy's visit on the day before his assassination in Dallas, buildings and markers commemorate events. Just a few of the notable structures will be mentioned here. They are readily available to view or visit during a stay in the city.

Courthouse

The Renaissance Revival style of this historic building marks the western end of Main Street with a clear vista to the Convention Center at the opposite extreme of downtown Fort Worth. Built between 1893 and 1895 using native red (it looks pink in the sunlight) granite and marble, it was designed to resemble the State Capitol in Austin. Adjacent court buildings, of a more recent vintage, were painted in *tromp l'oeil* manner to reproduce the granite block appearance of the Courthouse.

100 West Weatherford Street   817-884-1111
Fort Worth, Texas 76106

Fort Worth Courthouse

Will Rogers Center and Coliseum

This vast complex of meeting rooms, exhibit halls, animal barns, and coliseum takes up most of the land between Casa Manana and the Fort Worth Museum of Science and History. It is the site of the annual Fort Worth Livestock Show and Rodeo (usually held at the end of January), as well as numerous other animal competitions, rodeos, circuses, and conventions. The complex faces the Amon Carter and Kimbell Museums and features a bronze statue of Will Rogers astride his horse. Pioneer Tower accents its Art Moderne style. This area is known as Amon Carter Square. Will Rogers, the famous cowboy-humorist, and Carter (more about *him* later) were close friends.

The facility was constructed in 1936 under the supervision of Fort Worth architect Wyatt C. Hedrick. With Carter's influence, the Fort Worth Livestock Exposition was moved to the Will Rogers Center and has been held there every year since 1944.

Will Rogers on Soapsuds in front of the Pioneer Tower

One Amon Carter Square   817-871-8150
3301 West Lancaster Avenue
Fort Worth, Texas 76107

Thistle Hill

As the residential heart of the city spread south and west in the 1880s and 1890s, wealthy members of Fort Worth society built imposing homes for themselves and their families. Perhaps the most impressive of those still standing, in an area once called "The Summit," is Thistle Hill. It was built in 1903 as a wedding gift by cattle baron W. T. Waggoner for his daughter, Electra, and her Philadelphia socialite husband, A. B. Wharton. Could they have chosen Pennsylvania Ave. because Wharton came from that state?

The Neoclassical/Georgian Revival mansion faces Summit Avenue and is surrounded today by commercial buildings and hospitals. It is open as a museum and for tours.

1509 Pennsylvania Avenue   817-336-1212
Fort Worth, Texas 76104
Monday-Friday 10 A.M.-3 P.M., Sunday 1-4 P.M.

Eddleman-McFarland House

Another historic architectural gem of somewhat older vintage than Thistle Hill, this Victorian castle was new in 1898. It is made of yellow brick trimmed with red sandstone and sports a copper roof. Fort Worth's Junior League is headquartered here; tours are available.

1110 Penn Street   817-332-5875
Monday-Friday 10 A.M.-2 P.M., Sunday afternoons

Pollock-Capps House

Right next door is a renovated Queen Anne house attributed to the same architect (Howard Messner) as the Eddleman-McFarland. It is of red brick with white limestone trim and is in use as private offices.

Farther to the south, in Ryan Place, the Elizabeth Avenue Historic District boasts an array of beautiful period homes from the early part of this century (1911-1920). They are lovingly maintained, and many are on the National Register. Numerous other residential sections of Fort Worth (Berkeley, Park Hill, Mistletoe Heights, and Fairmount) are also involved in active programs of historic preservation.

1120 Penn Street

Marty V. Leonard Community Chapel

Lena Holston Pope, aided by a Sunday school class from Broadway Baptist Church, undertook to provide help for children in trouble. The Lena Pope Home received its first childcare license in 1930. After outgrowing its facilities four different times, the Home arrived at its present location in 1950. With donated supplies, volunteer labor, and much love, its main two-story colonial structure was built overlooking the Interstate. Through the years it has grown and expanded its assistance. Annually, the center now provides residential and off-campus services including crisis intervention, parent education, emergency hotline, and family preservation activity for more than twenty-five hundred youths and their families.

Marty Leonard, daughter of Marvin Leonard—one of the founders of Leonard's Department Store (a Fort Worth landmark now, sadly, gone)—was a long-time supporter of the Lena Pope Home. When a group of her friends decided to surprise her with a fiftieth birthday gift of a chapel for the Home, their contributions provided the architectural design and part of the construction costs. The balance of more than $2 million was raised in the community. The structure's completion in 1990 brought national attention to Fort Worth. Architect E. Fay Jones, of Arkansas, received the American Institute of Architects Gold Medal in 1990. President George Bush made the presentation. That gave Fort Worth the distinction of having buildings designed by four such medalists. The other three are Philip Johnson, Louis Kahn, and I. M. Pei.

Although the interfaith chapel is primarily for the youth of the Home, it is available for weddings and other community functions.

The sharp-peaked roof, supported by repetitive crossbeams, is accented by a sixty-foot skylight, which allows for the play of brightness and shadow in a constantly changing natural serenade of light throughout each day of the year.

Marty Leonard's friends started out to commemorate her more than thirty years of dedication to the work of helping children. During those years—which continue still—Marty twice served as president of the board of directors. This magnificent memorial will sustain a giving spirit for decades to come.

At the Lena Pope Home   817-731-8681
Interstate-30 between Sanguinet and Hulen Streets
Tuesday-Friday 10 A.M.-4 P.M., Sunday (once each month) 1 P.M.-4 P.M.

Not all children will enjoy touring old houses. Some want more interactive or animated pastimes. Museums, parks, and wildlife await them. Coming up!

Chapter 3

Museums

Fort Worth's Cultural District, home to the Will Rogers Memorial Coliseum and Casa Manana, also provides ambulatory access to several of the Southwest's finest museums. Tucked away in almost hidden corners of the city, however, are other exhibits equally worthy of attention. Even long-time residents may be unaware of the existence of some of these interesting displays.

All the internationally renowned collections are located in Fort Worth's "Cultural District"—a region within walking distance of the Will Rogers Complex.

Philip Johnson and Louis Kahn, two of America's greatest architects, are well represented in Fort Worth, where two outstanding art collections are housed in buildings designed by these men.

Kimbell Art Museum

The Pennsylvania connection again asserted itself in 1972, when Philadelphia architect Louis I. Kahn designed a museum to house a diverse collection of European masterworks. Kahn's stature in the world of architecture approaches that of Frank Lloyd Wright. The Kimbell, his final project in a lifetime of achievement, displays its internationally known collection, as well as frequent traveling exhibitions, in natural light let in by dramatic three-foot-wide skylights that run along the crests of each of the six arched vaults making up the museum's galleries.

In 1998 the Kimbell received the American Institute of Architects' Twenty-Five Year Award. This is given to a building project between twenty-five and thirty-five years old that exemplifies enduring architectural value.

Kay Kimbell moved to Fort Worth from Sherman, Texas, in 1924. Because he and his wife, Velma Fuller Kimbell, had no children and shared a love for fine art, the fortune generated by his interests in grain milling, food processing, insurance, oil, and real estate went in its entirety to the museum.

Their personal collection formed the nucleus used by the Kimbell Art Foundation to build, according to Mr. Kimbell's bequest, "an art museum of the highest rank" in his adopted hometown. While continuing to expand its own collections, the Kimbell is perhaps best known for hosting some of the finest traveling exhibits in the world. Often, these showings make only five or six stops in the United States. And, always, this is the Texas location of choice.

There is a special attention to piquing the interest of youngsters with the Kidstuff Program, which features a treasure hunt through the collections. In addition, the Buffet

Restaurant serves an excellent and reasonably priced lunch in the Maillol Courtyard. For parents, on Friday evenings, wine and a light buffet dinner may be had to the accompaniment of live jazz. Wine for the grown-ups, food and culture for all.

3333 Camp Bowie Boulevard   817-332-8451
Fort Worth, Texas 76107-2695   (Metro 817-654-1034)
www.kimbellart.org   FAX: 817-877-1264
Hours: Tuesday, Wednesday, Thursday, Saturday 10 A.M.-5 P.M.
Friday Noon-8 P.M., Sunday noon-5 P.M.
Closed: Thanksgiving Day, Christmas Day, New Year's Day, July 4th
Admission Free for permanent collection
Variable charges for special exhibits
Lunch: Tuesday-Thursday and Saturday 11:30-2:00
Friday and Sunday 12:00-2:00
Beverages and dessert: Tuesday-Sunday 2:00-4:00
Evening buffet: Friday 5:30-7:30

Amon Carter Museum

Philip Johnson, the New York City architect whose Texas designs include The Crescent in Dallas, shared in the layout of the Water Gardens and drew the plans for the Amon Carter Museum. When Amon Giles Carter Sr. died on June 23, 1955, he left a legacy in Fort Worth that far exceeded his fortune.

Opened in 1961 to showcase Mr. Carter's collection of mostly western art—highlighted by the works of Frederic Remington (1861-1909) and Charles Russell (1864-1926)— The Amon Carter Museum was enlarged in 1964 and 1977 with wings restricted to use by art historians and researchers. Its collection has focused on paintings, drawings, documents, and photographs pertaining to the western United States.

It has, in addition, an excellent selection of western bronzes. Remington and Russell predominate, but the museum has

Remington Sculpture at entry to the Amon Carter Museum

begun expanding its collection to include works by American artists of all periods and from all parts of the country. There are works by Georgia O'Keefe, Thomas Eakins, and Winslow Homer, as well as photographs by Eliot Porter. Other less well known but equally talented artists are also represented.

The Amon Carter is now undergoing renovations and is closed until sometime in 2001. Plan to come back. It will be worth the trip! In the meantime, check out the Amon Carter downtown, described at the end of this chapter.

3501 Camp Bowie Boulevard   817-738-1933
Fort Worth, Texas 76107-2695   www.cartermuseum.org
Hours: Tuesday-Saturday 10 A.M.-5 P.M., Sunday noon-5 P.M.
Closed: Mondays, New Year's Day, July 4, Thanksgiving Day, and Christmas Day
Admission: Free

Museum of Science and History

A short walk from the Kimbell, diagonally across the massive parking lot beside the Will Rogers Center (FREE surface and paid underground parking), is the Science Museum.

Of 1954 vintage, it is the oldest museum in the district and features exhibits on human biology, geology, anthropology, and computer science. Its history goes back even further.

The first charter for an association to administer a Children's Museum was granted in 1941. The museum opened in two rooms of the De Zavala Elementary School in 1945, moving two years later to the R. E. Harding House at 1306 Summit Avenue. A $500,000 bond sale financed the construction of the present building. In 1955 it added the Charlie Mary Noble Planetarium, the first to be named for a woman. The current name was adopted in 1968, and the Omni Theater came in 1983.

More than a million visitors a year participate in educational and entertainment activities at the Museum of Science and History, making it the most popular cultural attraction in North Texas.

Activities for children include:

Dino Dig

In this entry court, children of all ages can excavate fossil reproductions under the watchful gaze of a life-size model of a Tenontosaurus dossi, a dinosaur that lived in this area during the Cretaceous period. Its fossil remains, unearthed in Weatherford, are on display inside in the Lone Star Dinosaur exhibit.

Kidspace

Developed by the Ohio Center of Science and Industry and funded in part by a grant from the National Science Foundation, this part of the museum is reserved for children six years old and under (accompanied by their favorite grown-ups). Here youngsters learn by doing through activities such as Puppet Theater, Water Works, and Build-A-House.

Hands on Science

This is Kidspace for older children (over six). In a two thousand square-foot section of the museum lower level the museum staff provides numerous opportunities for building, dismantling, and studying objects, machines, and phenomena such as magnetism, gravity, balance, and momentum. It is open daily from 3 P.M. until museum closing and all day Saturday and Sunday.

Hands on History

Here, amid relics of the "Old West" visitors can examine and try on boots, chaps, and other items of cowboy clothing. Children can sit on a real saddle. Exhibits include branding irons, spurs, barbed wire, guns, and photos of cowboys in modern, traditional, and *vaquero* garb.

Museum School®

Accredited by the National Academy of Early Childhood Programs, Museum School® provides educational experiences for more than eighteen hundred children of preschool and school age every year. Using hundreds of items from the Museum collection, it gives them a chance to develop and satisfy a growing curiosity about our world from prehistory to the space age.

Omni Theater

The Omnimax® screen is a dome eighty feet in diameter, the BIGGEST in Texas, on which images from the largest film format in the history of photography are projected, taking the viewer almost literally into the picture. Seventy-two speakers provide sonic realism programmed to follow the action on the screen. The more than eight million people who have entered this first Omnimax® Theater in Texas have seen twenty-five different feature films.

Noble Planetarium

Now featuring a Spitz A3P star projector, a superb sound system, and multiple special effects projection units beneath a thirty-foot plaster dome, the planetarium has seating for eighty adults on an upholstered circular bench. The regular sky shows teach astronomy and related topics. Specials, keyed to various holidays, educate about such things as the "Star" the wise men may have seen at the time of the first Christmas.

1501 Montgomery Street   817-255-9300 or
Fort Worth, Texas 76107   Toll-free 1-888-255-9300
www.fwmuseum.org
Webteam: FWMSH1@metronet.com
Hours: Monday-Saturday 9 A.M.-9 P.M., Sunday noon-9 P.M.
Closed: Thanksgiving Day, Christmas Eve, Christmas Day

Admission:	Museum	Omni Theater	Planetarium
Adult	$5.00	$6.00	$3.00
Senior (61+)	$4.00	$4.00	$3.00
Junior (3-12)	$3.00	$4.00	$3.00

Fire Station No. 1

Maintained as an annex of the Museum of Science and History, Fort Worth's first firehouse opened in 1907 and remained in operation until 1980. It now showcases "150 years of Fort Worth," a walking tour of the city's growth and development. At its location adjacent to City Center Tower I, it is accessible from inside the Tower with convenient parking in the City Center Garage.

Second and Commerce Streets (Northeast corner)   817-255-9300
Hours: 9 A.M.-7 P.M. daily
Admission: Free

Cattle Raisers Museum

When you want to find out about the history of the cattle raising business or life on the ranch, ask Dr. Cheri L. Wolfe. This charming transplanted West Virginian is the curator of a superb little museum located minutes from downtown Fort Worth. Enter the exhibit hall to see a diorama featuring "TEX" the talking longhorn. Here, you learn about life on the ranch in the early days of Texas statehood. Then stroll around the corner to find displays of spurs, saddles, branding irons, and learn how the cattle business grew in the southwest.

Talking mannequins describe details of branding and branding irons or tell of the days when rustlers stole calves. Video theaters provide interactive learning experience.

Prearranged tour groups can try a scavenger hunt through the museum. See if you can find the butterfly in the crazy quilt, or try to pick out Nolan Ryan's brand or the famous "running W" of the King Ranch.

A thirteen-minute production in the museum's Amon Carter Theater traces the development of the Texas and Southwestern Cattle Raisers Association and the beef industry. On the way out, be sure to pick up a copy of "Why Beef?" Perhaps you'll find a new recipe for the week ahead.

1301 West Seventh Street   817-332-7064
Fort Worth, Texas 76102-2665   FAX: 817-332-8523
www.cattleraisermuseum.org
Hours: Monday-Saturday 10 A.M.-5 P.M., Sunday 1-5 P.M.
Admission: Adults $3, Children (4-12) $1
Youth (12-18), Association members, and Seniors $2
Children under 4 and organized school groups get in free!

Modern Art Museum

Built in 1954, this museum takes up where its companions leave off, emphasizing abstract art of the twentieth century. The permanent collection is frequently supplemented by touring exhibitions. It has been at its present location for more than forty years but was chartered in 1892, making it the oldest art museum in Texas.

Designed by New York architect Herbert Bayer, the current building has almost outlived itself. Groundbreaking a few blocks away is sceduled to take place in the fall of 1999 for the construction of a more "modern" Modern. The new structure, designed by Japanese master architect Tadao Ando, will more than triple the size of the Modern Art Museum (MAM). The planned opening date is in the spring of 2002.

Models of the new museum are on display at the MAM now, and the new location opposite the Kimbell makes the design even more striking, recapitulating the gallery arches of the Kimbell in squared-off form.

Art Camp at the museum gives budding young artists the chance to develop their talent. They can also learn about art by making it. Plan ahead and register early, as classes fill up quickly.

Scheduled tours give museum visitors insight into the features of the collection. They are free of charge and begin at 2 P.M. each Saturday. No prior arrangements are necessary. Show up, listen, and learn.

1309 Montgomery (at Camp Bowie Boulevard)   817-738-9215
Fort Worth, Texas 76107   www.mamfw.org
Hours: Tuesday-Friday 10 A.M.-5 P.M.
Saturday 11 A.M.-5 P.M., Sunday 12-5 P.M.
Closed Mondays and holidays
Admission: Free

Modern at Sundance Square

In 4,650 square feet of the old Sanger Building, within walking distance of all downtown Fort Worth hotels, this annex of the MAM houses portions of the permanent collection. It also provides additional room for traveling exhibits. A third of the space is used for the gift shop–larger than the one at the main branch—where books, jewelry, educational toys, and other interesting items may be purchased.

410 Houston Street   817-335-9215
Fort Worth, Texas 76102   www.mamfw.org
Hours: Monday-Thursday 11 A.M.-6 P.M.
Friday-Saturday 11 A.M.-10 P.M., Sunday 1-5 P.M.
Admission: Free

Tarrant County Historical Commission Museum

This is the museum that isn't. The room awaits the exhibits. The cabinets are built. But nothing's there. It is hoped that the displays will be in place before the end of the next millennium.

The Commission does maintain an extensive file of documents, clippings, and reference material in the courthouse annex next door. Helpful staff can direct groups to interesting sites around town, and arrangements can be made for Courthouse tours.

Hours: Any day, now

Antique Sewing Machine Museum

This is one of those "tucked away" places. Owner Frank Lee Smith and his daughter Halaina run the only museum of its kind in the United States. In 1996, to commemorate the sesquicentennial of Elias Howe's first practical sewing machine, he built the largest sewing machine in the world and now needs only cloth big enough to fit it. The needle is two feet long. The ten-foot machine, which actually sews, is a replica of an 1864 Civil War hand-cranked model and serves as the centerpiece of a display of all kinds of sewing devices.

Mr. Smith sings and composes country music. His musical selections are available on CDs at the museum. He also performs at private functions around the Metroplex and southern Oklahoma.

804 W. Abram   817-275-0971
Arlington, Texas 76013
Hours: Monday-Saturday 10 A.M.-5 P.M.
Admission: Adults $3, Children 5-16 $2, 4 and under free

Portraits of the Wild Zoo Gallery

Quick! Turn to Chapter 6. If you haven't been to the Zoo, now's the time to go, since this gallery is inside the Zoo grounds. At the present time the Gallery is reserved for private parties. Anyone about to have a birthday celebration? Be sure to make a day of it and combine the art viewing with a wildlife experience. The Gallery is located just inside the main gate near the gift shop.

1989 Colonial Parkway	817-871-7050
Fort Worth, Texas 76110	Hours: Same as the Zoo

Sid Richardson Collection

Oilman Sid Richardson (1891-1959) founded the family fortune that went to his great nephews (the Bass brothers). Like Amon Carter, he passionately pursued the works of Remington and Russell. Between 1942 and the year of his death, he was able to accumulate fifty-five of their paintings. The western themes depicted show real and fancied images of life in frontier times.

The collection went on display in 1982. It is located in Sundance Square near other Bass family holdings.

309 Main Street
Fort Worth, Texas 76102
www.sidrmuseum.org
E-mail: info@sidrmuseum.org
Hours: Tuesday, Wednesday 10 A.M.-5 P.M.
Thursday, Friday 10 A.M.-8 P.M., Saturday 11 A.M.-8 P.M.
Sunday 1 P.M.-5 P.M.
Closed Monday and major holidays
Admission: Free

817-332-6554
Toll Free: 1-888-332-6554
FAX: 817-882-9215

Arlington Historical Society

Founded in 1887 as the Cemetery Society, the Arlington Historical Society's mission is preservation of the cultural heritage of Arlington. The society maintains and operates the Fielder House Museum and the M. T. Johnson Plantation Cemetery and Historic Park. At both locations the Society presents tours for school children and other interested groups.

Colonel Middleton-Tate Johnson donated the land on which the Tarrant County Courthouse stands and is known as the "Father of Tarrant County." Johnson County is named for him. He and his family are buried in the Historical Park and Cemetery bearing his name.

Several historic buildings located on the grounds give the public a chance to feel the flavor of life in the early days of the region.

A quilt exhibit, held annually at the Fielder House since 1985, has displayed hundreds of quilts made or owned by Arlington residents.

1616 West Abram Street   817-460-4001
Arlington, Texas 76013   Hours: By Appointment

Arlington Museum of Art

The Arlington Art Association acquired an old J. C. Penney's department store in 1990 and turned itself into the Arlington Museum of Art. This step in the renovation of downtown Arlington produced a place for aspiring artists to display their work and for families to learn and share in the artistic experience.

With its ten changing exhibitions, the museum seeks to educate, stimulate, and demonstrate the intricacies of contemporary art. It holds discussion groups, gallery tours, classes, and free family activities.

Summer art camps, gallery scavenger hunts, and the fall basement haunted house keep the community youth interested. Membership in the museum association bestows some benefits and advantages, including gift shop discounts, receptions with the artists, and special programs and parties.

201 West Main Street   817-275-4600
Arlington, Texas 76010
Hours: Wednesday-Saturday 10 A.M.-5 P.M.
Admission: Free

Imagisphere Children's Museum

This nonprofit education center is supported by local industry and staffed by volunteers. In its new location at North Hills Mall—opened on July 6, 1999—it provides a place where children can expand their horizons. With exhibits on such varied subjects as sound, gravity, TV, technology, and the rainforest and *NO* "Do not touch" signs, it is a place to explore and try and do.

The ImagiVan is a mobile museum that visits schools and day care centers as well as birthday parties and corporate family events. The first exhibit, "How We See the World," demonstrates the physics of light, color, and optics. Three other mobile exhibits are in the planning stages.

7624 Grapevine Highway   817-589-9000
in North Hills Mall between food   www.imagisphere.org
courtyard and Mervyn's
North Richland Hills, Texas 76180
Hours: Tuesday-Saturday 10 A.M.-7 P.M., Sunday noon-6 P.M.
Closed Mondays
Admission: Adults and children 2 and over $3, 1-year-olds $1

Contemporary Art Center of Fort Worth

A recent addition to the Fort Worth art scene, this museum, founded in 1996, promotes the work of local and regional artists.

500 Commerce Street   817-877-5550
Suite 104   www.fwart.org
Fort Worth, Texas 76102
Hours: Wednesday-Saturday 11 A.M.-6 P.M.
Sunday noon-5 P.M.

Evelyn Siegel Gallery

Although not really a museum, this fine art gallery displays (for sale) such an exceptional range of works in a variety of media—from paintings to sculpture, carving to basketry— that it is a worthwhile stop even if you are not in the market for expensive home décor.

710 Montgomery Street   817-731-6412
Fort Worth, Texas 76107
Hours: Tuesday-Friday 11 A.M.-5 P.M., Saturday 11 A.M.-4 P.M.

National Cowgirl Museum and Hall of Fame

Another museum that isn't. *Yet*. But they're working on it and by the time this book gets to its second or third edition there'll be an update.

Visit the office to see an exhibit of Dale Evans' movie costumes and chat with the knowledgeable staff about our western heritage and the proposed museum. It will not only honor ranch women and cowgirls, but also writers, artists, teachers, and entertainers.

The gift shop sells memorabilia and western items seven days a week.

111 W. 4th Street   817-336-4475
Suite 300   www.cowgirl.net
Fort Worth, Texas 76102
Gift Shop hours: Monday-Friday 9 A.M.-5 P.M.

White Settlement Museum

This quaint eclectic collection includes several frontier vintage buildings as well as farm implements, a blacksmith shop, and furnishings, some of which date to the city's founding. There is an excellent research library and many photographic and equipment displays relating to the aircraft industry, which has played such an important role in Fort Worth's history. The city of White Settlement lies at the western edge of Fort Worth and was founded at almost the exact same time.

Grant Jackson and Jim Weaver give excellent guided tours of the buildings and grounds. Their conversational lectures are filled with anecdotes of events of the distant and recent past, including some in which they, themselves, took part.

White Settlement Historical Society   817-246-9719
Grant Jackson, President
8320 Hanon Drive
White Settlement
Fort Worth, Texas 76108
www.texasconnection.com/wsmuseum
Hours: Sunday 1-4 P.M. Or by appointment.
School groups welcome.
Admission: Free (donations accepted)

Historical Arms Museum

This small museum, located three miles southwest of Mansfield, features the N. R. Waters collection of firearms and other weapons. Included are European and Far Eastern matchlock and flintlock rifles as well as Japanese swords and other WWII memorabilia. There are also art works from around the world and mounted wildlife specimens from North America and Africa.

It is open for private tours by appointment only. Call for information.

4632 CR 617   817-473-3004
Mansfield, Johnson County, Texas 76063   Night/FAX: 817-473-1855

Stockyards Museum

Located in the Livestock Exchange Building, North Main Street in the Stockyards District, the museum showcases the collection of the North Fort Worth Historical Society. With photographs, plaques, and exhibits it depicts the early days of the city and the role of the cattle industry in the growth of Fort Worth.

You can view some of the photographs on the Virtual Texan website. Look in the menu under History and then scroll down to Stockyards Museum.

With the exception of Sarah Biles, museum director, the Stockyards Museum is staffed entirely by volunteers.

131 E. Exchange Avenue   817-625-5087
Fort Worth, Texas 76106   FAX: 817-625-5083
www.virtualtexan.com/comm/virtual/nswhs.htm
Hours: Monday-Saturday 10 A.M.-5 P.M.
Closed Sunday
Admission: free (Donations accepted)

Origins of the Southwest Museum

One more museum in the planning stages, this will begin fund-raising and construction in the near future. A planned exhibit in conjunction with The Smithsonian is to be held soon at the Legends of the Game Museum at the Ballpark in Arlington.

3825 W. Green Oaks Blvd.   817-465-5920
Fort Worth, Texas

Tarrant County Black Historical and Genealogical Society

A small exhibit is on view at Town Center Mall, and the archives are now at the Central Branch of the Fort Worth Public Library. Lenora Rolla, a spry ninety-five-year-old, is the historian and leads church and school groups through the display by appointment.

Town Center 4200 South Freeway   817-332-6049
Fort Worth, Texas 76115

Amon Carter Downtown

During the period of renovation on the Amon Carter Museum, there is a small downtown location across the street from Bass Hall. Twenty-five to thirty works are on display, and the bookstore sells art-related items. It will remain in operation until the main museum reopens, perhaps longer.

500 Commerce Street   817-738-1933
Fort Worth, Texas 76102
Hours: Tuesday-Wednesday 10:30 A.M.-5 P.M.
Thursday-Saturday 10:30 A.M.-8 P.M., Sunday noon-5 P.M.
Admission Free

Chapter 4

Aviation and Transportation

There are so many museums in the North Texas area dedicated to airplanes and other forms of transportation, that they deserve a chapter all their own. In the region centered on Fort Worth and Dallas, at least a dozen collections and related attractions have aviation as their main theme. Here are a few.

American Airlines C. R. Smith Museum

Between 1926 and 1933 several aviation companies served to carry mail, cargo, and passengers around the United States. In 1930 a number of these subsidiary carriers consolidated to form American Airways. In 1933 American began flying the Curtiss Condor, the first planes to carry stewardesses. The company changed its name to American Airlines, Inc., and in October 1934 Cyrus Rowlett Smith was named president.

Smith served until 1968, except for a stint as deputy commander of the Air Transport Command in World War II. He attained the rank of major general, and Lyndon Johnson appointed him secretary of commerce in 1968.

Born in Minerva, Texas, September 9, 1899, and educated in business administration, economics, and law at the University of Texas at Austin, Mr. Smith became an accountant with the Dallas firm of Peat, Marwick, and Mitchell in 1924.

From there, he went to work for A. P. Barrett's Texas-Louisiana Power Company. When Barrett entered the aviation industry, C. R. Smith went along. The rest is history.

C. R. Smith died in Washington, D.C., on April 4, 1990, and is buried in Arlington Cemetery.

The American Airlines C. R. Smith Museum opened in July 1993. Located a short distance southwest of D/FW Airport, it displays the DC-3 flagship *Knoxville*. Numerous other exhibits showing details of day-to-day operation give the visitor the opportunity to see, hear, and feel what goes on in the management of a major airline. With its IWERKS Theater and hands-on exhibits, there is something for everyone and every visit has something new.

4601 Highway 360 (at FAA Road)   817-967-1560
Fort Worth, Texas 76155   www.aa.com
Hours: Tuesday 10 A.M.-7 P.M., Wednesday-Saturday 10 A.M.-6 P.M.
Sunday Noon-5 P.M.
Closed: Monday, July 4ᵗʰ, Thanksgiving Day, Christmas Eve and Day,
Dec. 26, New Years Eve and Day, Jan. 2 and 3
Admission: Free

Aviation Heritage Museum

Little more than a fund-raising office now, but wait until the 171,000 square foot museum opens near Alliance Airport. In the meantime, plan to attend the annual International Airshow. In 1999 it was on October 9-10.

306 W. 7ᵗʰ Street   817-348-9900
Fort Worth, Texas 76101   www.aviationheritagemuseum.com

Pate Museum of Transportation

Planes, trains, and automobiles ought to be enough. But not at the Pate Museum. Here, miles from the sea, an MSB-5 mine sweeper boat cruises on dry land.

The auto collection ranges from a 1903 Cadillac to a 1981 Delorean and includes the rare 1937 V-12 Packard Club Sedan. There is also a London Double Decker Bus and a private railroad car fit for a president. In fact, the "Sunshine Special's Ellsmere" served as the private car for the president of the Texas and Pacific Railroad until it was presented to the Pate Museum.

The exhibit contains military aircraft, jet trainers and fighters, and several helicopters. A special feature is a full-scale mock-up of the Mercury Space Capsule.

| U.S. 377 between Fort Worth | 817-332-1161 |
| and Cresson, TX | 817-396-4305 |

Vintage Flying Museum

Doc Hospers brought home a B-17 Flying Fortress and named it "Chuckie" in honor of his wife. It serves as the centerpiece of a remarkable collection of over twenty World War II aircraft and a single lonesome jeep. In addition to the aircraft, there is an extensive reciprocal and jet engine exhibit room. In the hangar with "Chuckie," one of a limited number of B-17s still in flying condition, the Texas Air Command keeps its collection of helicopters. There is a British Hawker Hunter parked near a Canadian version of the F-86 Sabrejet.

Inside the museum, displays of model planes and other memorabilia of the war in Europe compete with an excellent gift shop where wind chimes made of .50 caliber machine gun shell casings hang beside the requisite T-shirts.

The VFM partners with the FAA to develop educational programs for students and teachers in the local school system.

505 NW 38th Street   817-624-1935
Hangar 33s   www.vintageflyingmuseum.org
Meacham Airport
Fort Worth, Texas 76106

Hours: Saturday 10 A.M.-5 P.M., Sunday 12-5 P.M.
Weekdays and group tours by appointment
Admission: $4 donation

The Vintage Flying Museum is host to the OV-10 Bronco Association and the Texas Air Command

Cavanaugh Flight Museum

Another marvelous collection of flyable aircraft ranging from those used in WWI through the Vietnam conflict, including the Sopwith Camel and a 1350-mph MIG-21. Come on a weekend and you are likely to see one or more of them in the air. Look for the F4 Phantom and stop in the Art Gallery to trace the chronology of aviation through paintings and photographs. An excellent gift shop offers educational and collectible items for enthusiasts of all ages.

Addison Airport   972-380-8800
4572 Claire Chennault
Dallas, Texas 75248
Hours: Monday-Saturday 9 A.M.-5 P.M., Sunday 11 A.M.-5 P.M.
Admission: Adults $5.50, Children, 6-12 $2.75, 5 and under free

Frontiers of Flight Museum

A full-scale model of the Sopwith *Pup* hanging outside the doors alerts you to the location of this collection. Inside, follow the history of the development of powered flight from the days before the Wright brothers to the Space Shuttle. In the course of this visit it will become clear why Dallas/Fort Worth deserves its reputation as the Aviation Capital of the World.

Dallas Love Field   214-350-1651
Love Field Terminal
Lobby, 2nd Floor, LB-18
Dallas, Texas 75235
Hours: Daily 9 A.M.-5 P.M., Sunday 1 P.M.-5 P.M.

Admission: Adults $2, Children, 12 and under $1
Members free

DFW Wing of the Confederate Air Force

A frequently changing collection of flyable WWII planes and a large display of memorabilia and artifacts. Other Wings of the Confederate Air Force contribute to the exhibit when their aircraft pass through this area. Membership in the CAF is open to those who wish to help preserve this heritage.

Lancaster Airport   972-617-7707 or
Beltline Road between I-45 and I-35E   972-227-9119
Hours: Saturdays 8 A.M.-5 P.M.
Admission: $1

Chapter 5

Parks, Playgrounds, Public Gardens

Botanic Garden

This one-hundred-nine-acre wonderland contains over twenty-five hundred varieties of native and exotic plants. A conservatory designed in 1986 by the Fort Worth firm of Hahnfield and Associates houses orchids and bromeliads in addition to other tropical and subtropical flowers and trees. It also provides rooms for educational activities and club meetings for organizations such as the Fort Worth Orchid Society. Here the novice can learn about plants. The experienced grower can exchange ideas and even obtain new specimens for his or her own greenhouse.

The Japanese Garden is a particular favorite of most visitors. The 1973 design of Denton, Texas architect Kingsley Wu, it was constructed on the site of an old gravel pit and transports the visitor to a six-acre parkland that recreates the Orient in the middle of Fort Worth. Filing along narrow, shaded paths, you may encounter a meditation garden or a teahouse. Then, a pagoda appears and waterfalls with pools in which swim imperial koi. Perhaps most impressive is the moon viewing deck.

Another floral wonder is the rose garden, which dates from 1934. Here, amidst a diversity of architectural settings, thousands of magnificent blooms representing dozens of rose varieties fill the air with their heady perfume and please the eye with their beauty. Local professional and amateur photographers regularly bring families and wedding parties for outdoor portraiture.

Topiary Longhorn at Botanic Garden

Frog Fountain at Botanic Garden

Heron statue at Botanic Garden

Each summer the Botanic Garden hosts a music festival—
Concerts in the Garden—which offer surprises and delight

for all when Independence Day approaches and lasers or fireworks are added to the music.

3220 Botanic Garden Boulevard   Japanese Garden Ticket Office:
Fort Worth, Texas   817-871-7685
817-871-7689   Gardens Restaurant:
Programs, Workshops, and Tours: 817-731-2547
817-871-7682
http://ci.fort-worth.tx.us/fortworth/pacs/botgarden/index.htm
Hours: Daily, 8 A.M.-11 P.M., Admission: Free
Conservatory: Monday-Friday, 10 A.M.-9 P.M.
Saturday, 10 A.M.-6 P.M. (4 P.M., November-March)
Sunday, 1-6 P.M. (4 P.M., November-March)
Admission: Adults, $1, Seniors and Children, 4-12, $.50
Children under 4, Free
Japanese Garden: April-October, 9 A.M.-7 P.M., Daily
November-March, 10 A.M.-5 P.M., Tuesday-Sunday, Closed Monday
Admission: $2, Weekdays, $2.50, Weekends and Holidays
Seniors, $.50 off regular admission, Children (4-12), $1; (under 4),
Free
Gift shop hours: Monday-Saturday, 10 A.M.-4 P.M., Sunday, 1-4 P.M.
Closed Mondays, November-March

Log Cabin Village

Travel a short distance south on University Drive from the Botanic Garden and a dilemma presents itself. Left into the Zoo? Or right to the Log Cabin Village? Do the Village and save the Zoo for a full day. Nestled among the trees of Forest Park is a group of seven log homes built in the 1850s by the pioneers who chose to reside in the Cross Timbers area just west of Fort Worth. They have been carefully moved from their original sites and lovingly restored. Furnished with authentic period artifacts, the cabins give a realistic flavor of life on the Indian frontier. Members of the Texas Senior Employment Program dress in costumes of the time and give demonstrations of candle making, corn milling, and other crafts and daily chores.

2100 Log Cabin Lane   817-926-5881
University Drive and Log Cabin Lane
Fort Worth, Texas
Hours: Tuesday-Friday, 9 A.M.-5 P.M.
Saturday, 10 A.M.-5 P.M., Sunday, 1-5 P.M.
Closed Monday
Admission: Adults, $2, Children, 3-11, and Seniors, $1.50

Trinity Park

Stretching for two miles along the west bank of the Clear Fork of the Trinity River, the gently rolling greenbelt of Trinity Park contains several miles of walking trails and crosses University Avenue to the Botanic Garden (described above).

Every year, at the end of April, the park is filled with merriment as Mayfest brings rides, games of chance, educational exhibits, and performers on multiple stages throughout the weekend.

And food. Don't forget the food!

Each year, during June and July, Trinity Park brings a spot of Elizabethan culture to Fort Worth with the Shakespeare in the Park program.

Duck Pond in Trinity Park. Photo courtesy of J. Reagan Ferguson.

2401 University Drive
Fort Worth, Texas

Water Gardens

See Chapter 1.

1502 Commerce

Handicap access

Built almost entirely by volunteer labor, this playground is a prototype for many that have sprung up in the past several years. It allows able-bodied parents to play with physically handicapped children. Perhaps more important, it also allows handicapped adults access to the play areas for their youngsters, whether handicapped or not.

Le Blanc Park
Granbury Rd. Cutoff between Granbury Rd. & Hulen Bend

Neighborhood Parks

Scattered throughout the city, within easy reach of foot and stroller traffic, there are numerous recreational areas for families with young children. Most have picnic facilities and practically every one has a playground. Other amenities include bike or hiking trails, baseball or soccer fields, basketball or tennis courts, and public swimming pools. Phone the Parks and Community Services Department (817-871-7275) for specifics.

Some of the community parks and centers are:

Arrow S. Park	7900 Cahoba Drive
Bradley Community Center	2601 Timberline Drive
Buck Sansom Park	3600 Angle Avenue
Carter Park	1300 East Seminary/ Carter Park Drive
Casino Beach Park	7500 Watercress Drive
Cobb Park	1600-3000 Cobb Drive
Como Community Center	4900 Horne Street
Diamond Hill Park and Community Center	1701 Northeast 36th Street
Dutch Branch Park	Dutch Branch Road east of Bryant Irvin
Fire Station Park and	Community Center
Forest Park	1500-2000 Colonial Parkway
Gateway Park	750 North Beach, 4501 East First Street
Greenbriar Park and Community Center	5200 Hemphill, 520 James St.
Hallmark Park	502 Sycamore School Road
Handley Park	2700 Haynie
Handley-Meadowbrook Community Center	6201 Beaty
Harmon Field	1601 Cypress
Bertha Collins Community Center	1501 MLK Boulevard
Heritage Park	300 North Main

Charles Haws Athletic Center	600 Congress Street
Highland Hills Park/ Community Center	1600 Glasgow Road
Hillside Park/ Community Center	1301 East Maddox
Lake Como Park	3401 Lake Como Drive
Marine Park	303 N.W. 20th Street
Marion Sansom Park	2300-2500 Roberts Cut Off
Martin Luther King Park/ Community Center	5565 Truman Drive
Far Northside Park/ North Tri-Ethnic Com. Ctr	2950 Roosevelt Avenue
Northside Park/ Community Center	1951 Lagonda/1801 Harrington Avenue
Oakland Lake Park	1645 Lakeshore Road
Oakmont Park	5500 Bellaire/6200 Bryant Irvin Road
Pecan Valley Park	Pecan Valley Drive
Prairie Dog Park	5000 Parker Henderson Rd.
R. D. Evans Community Center	3200 Lackland Avenue
Riverside Park	501 Oakhurst Scenic Drive
Riverside Community Center	201 South Sylvania Avenue
Rockwood Park	1851 Jacksboro Highway and University
Rolling Hills Park	2625 Joe B. Rushing Road
Rosemont Park & McLeland Tennis Center	1600 Seminary Drive
Southside Community Center	959 East Rosedale
Southwest Community Center	6300 Welch Avenue
Sycamore Park and Community Center	2525 East Rosedale
Sylvania Park & Riverside Community Center	3700 East Belknap
Thomas Place Park & Community Center	4231 Lafayette
Trail Drivers	1700 Northeast 28th Street
Trinity Park and Botanic Garden	2401 University Drive

Worth Heights Community Center	3551 New York Avenue
Z-Boaz Park (South)	5250 Old Benbrook Road

Golf Courses

The city of Fort Worth operates five golf courses. Nine others, privately owned, are open to the public. Junior golfers play at reduced rates on weekdays and after three P.M. on weekends. Call the individual courses for reservations and information.

Fort Worth City Courses

Meadowbrook	817-457-4616
1815 Jenson Road	
Pecan Valley	817-926-4653
6400 Pecan Valley Road	
Rockwood	817-624-1771
1851 Jacksboro Highway	
Sycamore Creek	817-535-7241
401 Martin Luther King, Jr. Freeway	
Z-Boaz Golf Course	817-738-6287
3240 Lackland Road	

Private courses (open to the public)

Carswell Golf Club	817-738-8402
6520 White Settlement	
Casino Beach Golf Course	817-237-3695
7464 Jacksboro Highway	
Fossil Creek	817-847-1900
3401 Clubgate Drive	
Glenn Garden Country Club	817-535-7582
2916 Glen Garden Drive	
Ideal Golf Course	817-572-7312
5151 Mansfield Highway	
Ironhorse	817-485-6666
6200 Skylark Circle, North Richland Hills	
Lake Arlington	817-451-6101
1516 W. Green Oaks Blvd., Arlington	

Lost Creek   817-244-3312
4101 Lost Creek Blvd., Aledo
Timber View   817-478-3601
4508 East Enon Road

Sculpture

Downtown Fort Worth

Until 1999, when the owners of the Bank One Building spirited it away, there was a giant red Alexander Calder eagle right in the middle of downtown. The uproar when it disappeared has not died out, but no one knows where it is now. It is rumored to be in New York, no, Philadelphia. That leaves us one piece poorer, but not by any means destitute. Statuary of all kinds can be found all around.

In Burnett Park the Matisse Backs intrigue passers-by. The four high relief sculptures were the gift to the city of the Tandy Foundation in 1984. They honor Anne Burnett Tandy. The park, with its bubbling waterways and spraying fountains, is a cool oasis in the heart of downtown.

Will Rogers Complex

Will sits astride his horse Soapsuds at the front entrance to the Coliseum, which bears his name. The statue, done by Electra Waggoner Biggs, brought two presidential families to Fort Worth in 1947. Dwight David Eisenhower dedicated it (that was *before* his presidency). Margaret Truman sang at the event (that was *during* her father's presidency).

Will, however, is not alone. Walk around the complex and other riders can be found. At the rear, near University on the Harley Avenue side of the complex, John Justin rides Baby Blue. Mr. Justin is known throughout the state and most of

the boot-wearing world as the retired chairman of the Justin Boot Company. He has long been an important figure on the Stock Show Board of Directors.

At the entry to the Amon Carter Exhibit Hall, a bronc in bronze rids himself of the cowboy on his back. This is Midnight, bearing Jim McNabb's Door Key band, and dubbed "The World's Greatest Bucking Horse." Midnight was born in Canada in 1910. During his career on the American Rodeo Circuit from 1923 to 1933, only nine men succeeded in riding him. They do not include the one in this January 19, 1984, statue by Jack Bryant.

Museum of Science and History

At the lower level Harley Street entrance, the Turtle stretches her neck out of a shiny chrome shell. This trademark tells everyone where to enter for Museum School classes.

Amon Carter Museum

In the garden outside the front entrance to the Carter you can see the abstract bronze sculpture Upright Motives, by Henry Moore. A long sweep of lawn leads from the statuary to the museum entrance.

Kimbell Museum

At the entrance to the museum on Arch Adams Street, a massive statue has held its arms outstretched since 1981. This is Joan Miro's "Woman Addressing the Public."

Travel down Hulen Street toward Bellaire Drive, where the parking lot near Charleston's and the Tom Thumb supermarket holds Chris Navarro's 1990 statue of a bull elk. What's he doing in the heart of Fort Worth? Looking for cow elk?

Head out north to the Stockyards and a herd of Texas longhorns stand frozen in time as if escaped from the nearby slaughterhouse. Take home photographic memories of the little ones mounted on these bronze behemoths.

Another longhorn eludes a cowboy in front of the Cattle Raisers Museum on West Seventh Street.

Camp Bowie Boulevard

In front of the BelTexSan Gallery at 3340 Camp Bowie near the museum complex, a large mounted cowboy hides in the shrubbery. It is called "The Rustler" and is another work by Jack Bryant.

Follow Camp Bowie Boulevard to Veterans Memorial Park just east of Arlington Heights United Methodist Church. At Crestline Street between Thomas Place and Washington Terrace find a bronze tribute to those who gave their lives during World War I "In Flanders Field"—a 1987 work, entitled "Duty," by Dr. Barvo Walker, a local dentist.

At 5925 Camp Bowie, the Jackalope stands guard over a wonderful shop where plants and pots await the home gardener. This mythical creature could only exist in Texas, especially one this size. A short distance farther west,

glittering abstractions add a touch of whimsy to the 6333 shopping center.

Lancaster Avenue

As you cross the Lancaster Avenue Bridge over the Trinity, look for the relief sculpted longhorns on the railing. Continue east on Lancaster to Main Street, near the railroad station, where a monument to Alfred Hayne pays tribute to a hero of the city who lost his life saving a crowd from a fire.

Arlington

The Stallions at Lincoln Square at I-30 near Highway 157 deserve at least a passing glance as you drive by or stroll around. A spraying fountain surrounds three rearing horses. To find them, you must wend your way among the scattered shops and restaurants of Lincoln Square. In the course of the journey, keep an eye open for the concrete menagerie— lions and hippos and other zoo creatures small enough for the kids to sit on. Kodak Moments galore.

Las Colinas/Williams Square Mavericks

If you want to see more equine art and have the time for a drive, go east to Williams Square in Las Colinas—in Irving, not far from Texas Stadium—and get a look at a magnificent herd of bronze mavericks splashing through an artificial watercourse. While there, perhaps you'd like to shop or dine along the Mandalay Canal. If not, maybe just a ride in one of the water taxis would be fun for the youngsters.

Dallas: More Longhorns

In Dallas, near the Dallas Convention Center and City Hall, see another herd of bronze longhorns on a trail drive. This collection of seventy steers and watchful cowboys is the largest bronze sculpture in the world. But you knew everything has to be bigger in Texas!

Nearby, the Pioneer Cemetery holds numerous stone monuments marking the graves of early residents and settlers of Dallas.

Chapter 6

The Animal Kingdom

Fort Worth Zoo and Aquarium

This is the wildest place in Fort Worth. On any given day, the child in each of us will lose him- or herself in the wonder and variety of the animal kingdom represented here in one of the finest zoological parks in America.

The latest exhibit to open, Thundering Plains, takes the visitor back to the early days of the frontier West when bison covered the prairies from horizon to horizon. Here, you will find a herd of these magnificent animals living peacefully (?) with the endangered Mexican gray wolf and a flock of wild turkeys.

Do not, however, expect to see all the zoo offers in less than a full day. There are too many interesting exhibits and too many dietary diversions. This is a place to visit and revisit. It will make you glad you live here—if you do—and you'll want to return if you're from far away.

The Zoo offers special benefits to those who wish a yearly membership in its Safari Club. Levels of this membership impart increasing privileges to the dedicated Zoophile.

Zoo School

For children from two to six years of age, Zoo School provides educational experiences at various times throughout the year. Classes are divided into sessions for two-year-olds (each must be accompanied by an adult), three- & four-year-olds (must be potty-trained), and five- & six-year-olds. Safari club members may register early by returning forms no later than the Priority Registration date. Call the Education Department (817-871-7465) for details.

How to get there: From I-30, take University Avenue south to Colonial Parkway. The Zoo entrance is to the left.

1989 Colonial Parkway	Education Department: 817-871-7465
Fort Worth, TX 76110	Safari Club: 817-871-7019
817-871-7050	www.fortworthzoo.com

Hours: Daily 10 A.M.-5 P.M., Weekend hours extended seasonally
Admission: Adults $7, Children 3-13 $4.50, Seniors 65 and up $3
Toddlers 2 and under free
Parking: $3 On Wednesdays admission is half price and parking is free.

Fort Worth Nature Center and Refuge

The thirty-five hundred acres enclosed within this preserve make it the largest municipally owned wildlife sanctuary in the United States. Within its boundaries are twenty-five miles of walking trails through almost every type of natural habitat found in Texas. Along these, visitors may traverse river bottom, marsh boardwalk, fossil shell outcrop, and forested islands.

You will have the opportunity to view native flora and fauna, including the preserve's buffalo herd. Nature programs and recreational activities are available, geared for school groups of all ages, at the nominal cost of $2 per person.

You can enjoy excellent volunteer experience at the Nature Center.

How to get there: Take North Loop 820 to Highway 199 and go north about five miles.

9601 Fossil Ridge Road   817-237-1111
(Off Highway 199)
Fort Worth, Texas 76135
Hours: 9 A.M.-5 P.M. Daily
Visitor Center Hours: Tuesday-Saturday 9 A.M.-5 P.M.
Sunday noon-4:30 P.M.
Closed Monday
Admission: Free (Donations accepted)

Fossil Rim Wildlife Refuge Conservation and Learning Center

Deepest, darkest Africa—and that's not all—just fifty miles from Fort Worth. Here, on twenty-seven hundred acres, many endangered species from around the world roam free in an unspoiled habitat where man may visit and enjoy their splendor. And it's only an hour's drive from Fort Worth.

From its private beginning in the Texas Hill Country, Waterfall Ranch was in danger of failing several years ago. In 1987 it became Fossil Rim Wildlife Center and has now evolved into more than a tourist destination. Actively involved in conservation and captive breeding programs for numerous endangered species, it also has facilities for overnight stays in settings that transport the guest to wild regions of our globe. Whether you choose the luxury of The Lodge at Fossil Rim or Foothills Safari Camp with its air-conditioned tents, a vacation stay here will provide lasting memories.

Even if you only drive down for the day, the experience will imprint itself in your memory. Over eleven hundred wild animals range unrestrained through the park. Only the carnivores and rhinos are kept restricted. Active research on ocelot biology and rhino reproduction and nutrition are ongoing. Species survival plans for about a dozen different breeds are carried out in cooperative efforts with zoos and wildlife parks around the country.

Because a corporation runs Fossil Rim, it is well organized and offers numerous activities for visitors of all ages. The Overlook Café has light snacks and "hungry-man" lunches with indoor and outdoor seating and a view of the valley. Get souvenirs at The Nature Store. The Nature Trail and Petting Pasture will keep the youngsters happy.

More adventurous, active guests should try the half-day mountain bike tours, which start at 9 A.M. and 3 P.M. on selected weekends. The cost is $30 and trails are geared to the rider's skill.

There is a Wildlife Walk with an area for Pondside Picnics that accommodates groups of up to one hundred. The $3 fee can be applied to the $27 price of the Behind the Scenes Tour.

Conservation Camp is a fun experience for family groups and has day, overnight, and extended scheduled activities. Details about Day Camp and Family Camp are available by phone or at the center.

The basic visit is incomplete without the Scenic Drive. This nine-and-one-half-mile self-driven tour takes you through the park and gives glimpses, sometimes very close-up, of the varied wild life. Special rates are given to large children's and school groups.

How to get there: Take I-35 south from Fort Worth towards Cleburne. Exit on U.S. 67 westbound. Go through Glen Rose to Texas 2008 (approx. 3 mi.). Turn left. Park Entrance is on right (approx. 2 mi.). Look for stonework pillars.

P.O. Box 2189   254-897-2960
Glen Rose, Texas 76043-2189   www.fossilrim.com
Scenic Drive: Adults $14.95, Seniors 62 and up $11.95
Children under 12 $9.95

The Dallas Zoo and Dallas Aquarium

Where is the tallest statue in Texas? No, it's not Sam Houston on Interstate 45 near Huntsville. The sixty-seven-and-one-half-foot giraffe, created by award-winning St. Louis artist Bob Cassily, located at the entrance to the Dallas Zoo takes the prize.

If the Fort Worth Zoo isn't enough, or if you are closer to the east side, this wildlife experience offers an acceptable alternative. Check out the Lemur Lookout as you enter. The interactive Reptile Discovery Center highlights an outstanding reptile collection.

There is also a walk-through rain forest aviary and a twenty-five-acre Wilds of Africa exhibit containing ninety species of African birds and mammals in settings that replicate their natural surroundings in six different habitats. A mile-long monorail ride takes you over the varied enclosures to give an aerial view.

In 1997 the zoo completed a $1.9 million Chimpanzee Forest to show off these amusing, endangered animals.

The Children's Zoo offers youngsters up-close and personal wildlife experiences, and the Tom Thumb Pet Pal Central helps families choose the perfect pet for their needs.

650 South R. L. Thornton Freeway   214-670-5656
I-35 at Marsalis exit   www.dallas-zoo.org
Three miles south of downtown Dallas
Hours: 9 A.M.-5 P.M. Daily
Closed Christmas Day
Admission: Adults $6, Seniors 65 and up $4, Children 4-11 $3
Under 4 and Dallas Zoological Society Members Free
Parking $3 per car

The Dallas Aquarium at Fair Park

Close to the Texas Star Ferris wheel, the recently renovated aquarium building was originally constructed for the 1936 Texas Centennial. Although seven miles separate them, the Aquarium at Fair Park is administratively part of the Dallas Zoo.

Shark and piranha feedings should amuse even the most sedate child. They are held daily except Monday at 2:30 P.M. The electric eel exhibit will also prove to be a shocking experience.

The breeding lab provides an opportunity for observation of conservation efforts to save threatened species, such as the desert pupfish and the Texas blind salamander.

Educational programs for school-age children, from kindergarten through twelfth grade are held Monday through Saturday. Groups are limited to thirty students. The younger ones get to learn about fish and other aquatic life forms and their babies. The more mature can delve into lessons on anatomy and physiology, food chains and feeding habits, and occupational opportunities at zoos and aquaria.

Membership in the Dallas Zoological Society gives free admission to the Zoo and Aquarium all year. Call 214-943-2771 for information.

1462 First Avenue and Martin   214-670-8443
Luther King Boulevard   www.dallas-zoo.org
Dallas, Texas 75226
Hours: 9 A.M.-4:30 P.M. Daily
Closed Thanksgiving Day and Christmas Day
Admission: Adults $3, Children 3-11 $1.50, 2 and under free
Pre-registered school groups $.75 per person

Natural Bridge Wildlife Ranch

Take a safari, Texas style. This is closer to San Antonio than to Fort Worth, but is a worthwhile side trip if you plan a few days down that way. Stay in New Braunfels (see Chapter 17) and make this a day trip from there. Don't take the Rolls Royce, just in case the rhinos get playful.

Located in the Texas Hill Country near Natural Bridge Caverns north of San Antonio, another good destination, this ranch has been owned by the same family for more than one hundred years. It now shelters over fifty species, many of them endangered, from every continent except Antarctica, with constant additions. There is an active captive-breeding program; visitors can occasionally witness birth of new offspring.

How to get there: Approximately midway between New Braunfels and San Antonio off I-35. Take Exit 175 and travel northwest. If you come to Natural Bridge Caverns, you've gone too far.

26515 Natural Bridge Caverns Road   830-438-7400
San Antonio, Texas 78266   www.nbwildliferanchtx.com
Hours: 9 A.M.-5 P.M. Daily
Summer (Memorial Day-third weekend in August): 9 A.M.-6:30 P.M.
Closed Thanksgiving, Christmas, and New Year's Day
Admission: Adults $8.25, Seniors 65 and up $7.25, Children 3-11 $5.25

River Legacy Parks and Living Science Center

The Exhibit Hall admission allows free participation in the weekly nature hikes (meet in the Living Science Center Saturdays, 9:30-10 A.M.) and animal presentations (Saturday, 2 P.M.). The Center has a nature school for kids 3-5, and sponsors field trips for school children K-12th grade. Also available: Junior Naturalist Clubs and adult classes.

703 NW Green Oaks Boulevard   817-860-6752
Arlington, Texas 76
Hours: Tuesday-Saturday 9 A.M.-5 P.M., Sunday 1-5 P.M.
Admission: Adults $3, Children 2-18 $2, Under 2 free

Arbuckle Wilderness

A short distance north of the Metroplex off I-35 at Exit 51 is another game park similar to Fossil Rim. This one is in the picturesque Arbuckle Mountains of southern Oklahoma. The park is undergoing a change of ownership and major renovation, but it will remain open during the process.

Picnic meadows, paddleboats, and a go-cart track are among the activities families may enjoy in addition to watching and feeding the animals.

Route 1, Box 63   1-800 738-PARK (7275)
Davis, Oklahoma 73030
Hours: 9 A.M.-5 P.M. Daily
Admission: Adults $10.99, Children 3-11 $7.99, Under 3 free

Heard Natural Science Museum and Wildlife Sanctuary

This is a nature preserve and wild bird rehabilitation center in addition to a natural history museum. Located in McKinney, Texas, it is easily reached from anywhere in the Metroplex. And worth a trip.

One Nature Place   972-562-5566
McKinney, Texas 75069-9244   Raptor Centre: 972-562-5560
www.heardmuseum.org   FAX: 972-548-9119

International Exotic Feline Sanctuary

A different kind of wildlife preserve, dedicated to endangered and abused felines who have been in shows, zoos, or inappropriately kept as pets until they outgrew their cuddliness.

The sanctuary opened in 1988 to care for these cats and serves as an educational resource for the interested public. It provides a home for Amur leopards, bobcats, cougars, tigers, and many endangered species of the feline persuasion.

From Dallas: (approximately 50 miles) Take Hwy 114W past the north entrance to DFW Airport; follow signs toward Bridgeport—Hwy 114W and 81/287 merge briefly—take 114W to Bridgeport exit and turn left at the stop sign. IEFS is 3 miles ahead on the right.

From Fort Worth: (approximately 35 miles) Take 35W north to Hwy 81/287 toward Decatur. Take the Hwy 114W exit to Bridgeport. IEFS is 3 miles ahead on the right.

From Decatur: (approximately 15 miles) Take Hwy 81/287 south toward Ft. Worth. Take the Hwy 114W exit to Bridgeport. IEFS is 3 miles ahead on the right.

P.O. Box 637
Boyd, TX 76023
E-mail: info@bigcat.org

940-433-5091
Fax: 940-433-5092
www.teff.org

Chapter 7

Sports and Athletic Events

The Texas Rangers

In 1999 Nolan Ryan made the Baseball Hall of Fame. It's fitting he's the first Texas Ranger player to make it. In a career seeing him pitch for four different teams, Nolan Ryan played during more seasons than anyone in Major League Baseball history. He ended his career here.

With the completion of The Ballpark in Arlington on April 1, 1994, the Texas Rangers returned to the nostalgic setting of an old-time baseball stadium. Arlington Stadium served from 1965 to 1993. It cost $1.5 million to build and had 10,600 original seats. The Ballpark, thirty years later, cost $191 million and opened with 49,166 seats. It is the centerpiece of a two-hundred-seventy-acre complex and is surrounded by nine parking lots.

Fans of all ages find excitement and education here. The facility includes the Legends of the Game Baseball Museum and Children's Learning Center, Dr Pepper Youth BallPark, a twelve-acre lake and additional perimeter parks and recreation areas.

The Ranger players are active in the community, participating in numerous charitable fund-raising and public service events all year long.

Tours of The Ballpark in Arlington last fifty minutes. Tickets can be purchased separately or in combination with admission to the Museum. Discounts are available for groups of at least twenty-five. The Museum can also be rented for children's birthday parties and sleepovers for first-sixth graders. Call tour booking at 817-273-5099.

How to get there: Take I-30 east from Fort Worth or west from Dallas. Exit at Nolan Ryan Expressway (from the west) or Ballpark Way (from the east) and go south. The Ballpark is just north of Randol Mill Road. The Legends of the Game Museum is inside the Ballpark

The Ballpark in Arlington   817-273-5100
1000 Ballpark Way   www.texasrangers.com
Arlington, Texas 76011
Museum Hours:
April-October: Monday-Saturday 9 A.M.-6:30 P.M., Sunday 12-4 P.M.
November-March: Tuesday-Saturday 9 A.M.-4 P.M., Sunday 12-4 P.M.
Closed Monday

The Dallas Cowboys

"America's Team" has struggled in recent years, but no professional football club has been able to match the accomplishments of the Dallas Cowboys. Rebuilding continues and soon they'll be in contention for an eighteenth division title and, perhaps, a ninth trip to the Super Bowl.

As things stand, no other team has been in eight Super Bowls; none has won three in four years. The Cowboys and the San Francisco Forty-Niners are the only teams to win five Super Bowl Championships. No other NFL team ever won its division four years in a row. The Cowboys did that twice.

The Cowboys have been in almost one-fourth of all the Super Bowl games ever played, so there's a good chance they'll be back.

From 1960 to 1971, the team played in the Cotton Bowl. Construction of Texas Stadium began in 1969. The roof was deliberately left open so, as Texans love to say, "God could watch his favorite team." Seating capacity is 66,675 and the two giant DiamondVision TV screens allow instant replay viewing larger than life!

Texas Stadium in Irving has been home to the Cowboys since 1971. In the first game played there, the Cowboys beat the New England Patriots 44-21 on October 24, 1971. Since then, "Da Boys" have won three out of every four home games.

Tickets for individual games range in price from $36-$61. Tours of Texas Stadium are available at individual or group rates. A tour is included in the price of a party at the Stadium ($5/person for twenty-five or more people) which can be held on non-game days. Call 972-785-4780 for more information.

The Executive Chef, Michael Mudrone, and his staff of experts will cater gala functions at "slightly higher" prices. Call 972-785-4000 for more information.

Tour Schedule, on the hour:
Monday-Saturday 10 A.M.-3 P.M.
Sunday 11 A.M.-3 P.M. when there is no game.

How to get there: From Fort Worth or Dallas take Highway 183 east or west to Irving. Follow signs to Texas Stadium when you reach Loop 12 or Highway 114.

Texas Stadium   972-554-6368
201 E. Airport Freeway   FAX: 972-554-8336
Irving, Texas 75062
www.dallascowboys.com

The Dallas Mavericks

In a season that runs from November to mid-April, the Dallas Mavericks play eighty-two basketball games, half of them at 18,000-seat Reunion Arena.

Ticket prices range from $8-$85. Parking is $7 per car ($5 in Lot G). Arrive early! The lots fill quickly on game days, especially when the Chicago Bulls come to town.

Season and half-season tickets are available at package prices, and some seats are discounted to groups of twenty-four or more.

Arena tours and tours of the Mavericks locker room and gift shop take forty-five minutes and are free to groups of ten or more. Reservations must be made in advance (972-988-DUNK).

Reunion Arena
777 Sports Street
Dallas, Texas 75207

972-988-DUNK (3865)
www.nba.com/mavericks

The Dallas Stars

The Dallas Stars moved here from Minnesota (where they had been called the North Stars) and quickly made themselves at home. Their exciting style and high energy led to remarkable growth of ice hockey as a spectator sport in Texas. In 1999 they became World Champions, winning the Stanley Cup.

Between September and April, the Stars take the ice ninety-one times (nine pre-season and eighty-two regular season contests), about half of them at Reunion Arena. Season ticket prices range from $20 to $250 *per game.*

Home field for the Dallas Mavericks and the Dallas Sidekicks, as well as the Stars, Reunion Arena cost $27 million when it opened in 1980. The addition of a five-story parking facility in 1987 increased capacity to 6,400 cars. ٠

In a busy entertainment year, Reunion offers visitors numerous concerts—and the Circus—for those interested in watching something other than sports.

How to get there: Take Highway 183 east to I-35E South and exit at Reunion Boulevard.

Reunion Arena   214-GOSTARS (467-8277)
777 Sports Street   817-273-5100
Dallas, Texas 75205   For Group Ticket Sales:
www.dallasstars.com   214-868-2834

The Texas Motor Speedway

Ticket prices range from $16 to $66 at the Speedway box office (slightly higher at other locations such as Ticketmaster). Groups of at least twenty-five who purchase in advance get a discount.

The Texas Motor Speedway opened in 1997 with the NASCAR Coca-Cola 300 on April 5 and the NASCAR Winston Cup 500 on April 6. With more than 150,000 seats, and room for another 53,000 in the infield, there is ample opportunity for spectators to enjoy auto racing. To make it really interesting, try camping in the infield.

Speedway World, the gift shop located in the corporate office building, is the point of origin for tours of the second largest sports facility in the United States. (The largest is Indianapolis Motor Speedway.) Cost is $6 for adults and $4 for senior citizens and children under 13. They are offered year round, Monday-Friday 9 A.M.-4 P.M., Saturday 10 A.M.-4 P.M. and Sunday 1 P.M.-4 P.M.

Another fun event is the Thursday Night Stampede. This goes on during the summer and is an excellent place for a child's birthday celebration. For $15 per adult and $12 for each child under 13, parties include Legends race tickets, favors for the kids, a gift for the birthday child, hot dogs, soft drinks, chips, and a visit from Sparky, the official mascot. Make reservations at least a week in advance.

If you are particularly well heeled or have corporate connections, consider a membership in the Speedway Club.

This magnificent structure has a dance floor and a four-tiered dining room overlooking the Speedway. In addition, there are meeting and conference rooms, banquet and catering facilities, and a spa and fitness center. For the youngsters, while parents are occupied, the Little Legends Day Care will keep them happy and active.

How to get there: Leaving Fort Worth, go north 20 miles on IH-35W. Can't miss it.

3601 Highway 114	Mailing Address: P.O. Box 500
Justin, Texas 76247	Fort Worth, Texas 76101-2500
817-215-8500	www.texasmotorspeedway.com
Guest feedback: TMS Guest Feedback@texasmotorspeedway.com	

The Fort Worth Brahmas

It is no longer necessary to travel all the way to Dallas to see great hockey. The Brahmas, Fort Worth's *only* professional sports franchise, play at the Fort Worth Convention Center, except for the last two games, which are at the Will Rogers Coliseum.

Season ticket prices range from $315-$630. Ten-percent discounts are given for tickets purchased before September 1. Individual game tickets are $9-$18. There are twenty-six games on Friday nights, so more families can attend.

Andy Moog's Brahmas finished the 1998 WPHL season in the semifinals and plan to do better in 1999-2000. Fan participation is steadily growing, thanks in part to the antics of Bruiser, the team mascot, who cavorts in the stands during games.

Bruiser's Birthday Club makes a hockey game part of the celebration. For two-hundred dollars the party gets twenty tickets, a scoreboard announcement for the birthday child, cake, and a personal visit from Bruiser. For an additional two-hundred dollars, you can have a private room at the game with ice cream, soda, and pizza.

During the off-season, Brahma players remain involved in the community by teaching in the Blacktop Brahmas program. At twenty-two locations around the Metroplex, kids learn hockey basics on in-line or roller skates free of charge.

In addition, there is a "Grades for Blades" reward program, which gives free hockey tickets to students who excel in the classroom.

1314 Lake Street, Suite 200	817-336-4ICE (4423)
Fort Worth, Texas 76102	FAX: 817-336-3334
www.brahmas.com	

The Dallas Burn

Dallas Burn Soccer heats up the Cotton Bowl between April and October each year, with sixteen regular-season and a couple of international or exhibition games.

The Cotton Bowl will have its sixty-fifth birthday in the year 2000. The Burn can host a birthday party for fifteen or a corporate or soccer club banquet for more than a thousand. Either group will take lasting memories home. After the banquet, guests stay for the game. Call 214-979-0303 or E-mail mail@burnsoccer.com for details.

Burn Soccer has a unique community outreach program, which allows businesses in the Metroplex to donate tickets so underprivileged children can see a Major League Soccer contest. Package prices range from $550 to $2800 and provide four to twenty season tickets for charities to distribute.

Season tickets can be purchased for all, half, or one-third of the games and prices vary from $6 to $25 per game (single game tickets: $9 to $30). In addition, there is the Flexi-Pass. For $200 you get twenty vouchers redeemable for any game in any combination during the season. Go with a friend to ten games or use 'em all at once for a big party!

Kids interested in soccer might want to join the Kellogg's Rookie Prospect Club. They will receive a Dallas Burn T-shirt, two tickets to a Dallas Burn home game, and an invitation to Rookie Prospect Clinic, the official camp of the Dallas Burn. Membership charge is $14.

One more thing: KidZone on the Burn website will keep the computer-using youngsters busy *and* happy.

2602 McKinney Street, Suite 200
Dallas, Texas 75204
214-979-0303
FAX: 214-979-1188
www.burnsoccer.com
E-mail: mail@burnsoccer.com
Hours: Monday-Friday 9 A.M.-5 P.M.

Pro Shop
2602 McKinney Street
Dallas, Texas
214-979-0303
www.mlsnet.com

Dallas Sidekicks

The World Indoor Soccer League's North Texas representatives are the Sidekicks, playing home games at Reunion Arena. The season lasts from July until late November. There are fourteen home games with tickets from $5 to $25. Groups can get season ticket discounts.

Junior Sidekicks have some special advantages. For a $10 membership, they receive tickets to three games plus free decals, stickers, and a newsletter. There is also an opportunity to be an "Honorary Ballkid" and be introduced with the team. Discounts for Sidekicks Camp and Sidekicks Party Club are coupled with reduced prices on additional tickets for friends and family members.

Reunion Arena
77 Sports Street
Dallas, Texas 75205

www.sidekicks.com

Lone Star Park

During thoroughbred racing season, Lone Star Park provides a Family Fun Park to occupy the children of race fans. It includes a petting zoo, bounce buildings, and other kid-friendly activities. Moms and Dads are welcome.

1000 Lone Star Parkway	972-263-RACE (7223)
Grand Prairie, Texas 75050	www.lonestarpark.com

Marathons, Triathlons, Etc.

Races and group participation sporting events take place throughout the year all around the Metroplex. Most have some charitable organization as sponsor and beneficiary.

Some Examples:

Candlelighter Night Run

August 19, 2000 will be the fourth time the event has been held.

Benefiting Candlelighter Childhood Cancer Foundation and Cook Fort Worth Children's Hospital, it combines a 1K Fun Run and a 5K Run/Walk through downtown Fort Worth. Participants carry glow sticks to help promote Childhood Cancer Awareness Month in September.

Call 817-810-1382 or E-mail Candlerun@juno.com for details.

Bike to the Brazos

An annual event to benefit The Multiple Sclerosis Society, this 150-mile, two-day cycling tour goes from Fort Worth to Glen Rose and back each year in mid-September. Participants get sponsorships to help raise money for research and treatment of MS. The 2000 dates are September 16-17.

Call 817-877-1222 ext. 61 or 1-800-FIGHTMS or check the web: www.txms150.org or www.msbiketours.org. Contact the North Texas Chapter of the Multiple Sclerosis Society:

2501 Parkview Drive, Suite 550
Fort Worth, Texas 76102-5817

Numerous other races are held throughout the year, so someone's always running.

Jingle Bell Run

This one benefits the Arthritis Foundation. It is held each year on the Saturday following Thanksgiving in conjunction with the Downtown Fort Worth Parade of Lights and Christmas tree lighting ceremony and includes a 5K Night Run, 5K Fun Walk and 1 Mile Elf Run. Registration fees ($20 on race day, less in advance) aid arthritis sufferers and entitle participants to jingle bells and T-shirts commemorating the event.

Horseback Riding

This had to be included, right? The only problem is deciding where to do it. It won't matter where you live or stay. There will be a riding facility within reach. The following are typical of what is to be found. Check yellow pages for others (look under Horse and Stables).

Benbrook Stables

Coming into Benbrook on U.S. 377 from the south, visitors pass, often with the barest glance, Benbrook Stables. Molly and Steven Thompson took over the management in 1998 and infused it with love and labor—theirs and that of friends and volunteers—not to mention money. Now, their expanding business caters to riders from beginner to expert as well as horse owners.

Special activities for kids, and the occasional parent, include rides (trail, pony, and hay), camping, play days, riding lessons, and a day camp at various times during the summer months. Call Molly at 817-249-1001 for details and reservations. They also host birthday parties, horse shows and rodeos, and have facilities for corporate functions.

The Benbrook Stables Riding Club contributes a passel of ponies and riders of all ages to the Summerfest Parade, an annual Benbrook event that ends at dark with fireworks at Benbrook Lake. It is held the Saturday before the Fourth of July.

10001 U.S. 377 South   817-249-1001
Benbrook, Texas 76126

Park Ridge Stables

A few miles further north on Highway 377, more equine activity awaits. Doug and Susan Anderson welcome experienced riders and just-starting small fry. A basic introduction is the Field Trip, which features a tour of the grounds, education about horses, and a visit to the petting zoo. For a few dollars more the child can ride a horse and be photographed sitting on Romeo, the longhorn steer.

"Little Dudes and Dudettes" (ages 10 and under) and "Young Cowboys and Cowgirls" (ages 11-up) can have birthday parties at Park Ridge or—if Mom and Dad prefer—the party can come to you (one horse and the petting zoo). Be sure to have enough film for the family camera!

Options that can be added to basic party fixin's include a hayride, a weenie roast, hats, bandannas, badges, and a videotape memory.

In addition, if you have your own horse, they can assist with training and riding lessons or boarding.

6019 Highway 377 S.   817-377-8021
Fort Worth, Texas 76116   817-485-5101

Mad Ivan's Paintball

Tag, you're it! In this high-tech game, you'll know when you've been tagged. Wear old clothes and prepare to get dirty.

The minimum age to play is 10 years, with fathers and sons often teaming up. In a 37,000-square-foot indoor court, they compete to "capture the flag" or "free the captive teddy bear." Using special air guns, firing gelatin capsules containing a mixture of oil and water-soluble paint, at no more than 250 feet per second, the "combatants" tag each other until one team stands victorious.

Mad Ivan provides a video arcade, meeting area, snack and coffee bar, and observation ports for those who only want to watch.

The doors open at 6 P.M. on weekdays, 10 A.M. on Saturday, and noon on Sunday. Ivan goes home after the last paint ball breaks. The staff is knowledgeable, helpful, and experienced. Many are former Scouts. Safety rules are rigidly enforced.

Mad Ivan's rewards academic achievement and good citizenship with prizes and field passes.

How to get there: From I-35 exit at Berry. Go west to Cleburne Street. Turn right, then left on West Bowie. From I-30 or I-20 exit Forest Park south or McCart north. At Berry Street turn east to Cleburne Street. Then right and left as above.

1813 W. Bowie Street   817-923-6422
Fort Worth, Texas 76110   FAX: 817-923-6421
www.madivan.com
Field fee: $7, Paint: $8 per 100 rounds
Sharpshooter Pack: $17 (Field fee, Pump marker, Mask, 100 rounds)
Go Postal Pack: $27 (Field fee, Semi-auto marker, Mask, 100 rounds)
Group rates available for birthday parties, church and corporate groups, family reunions, and team challenges.

Golf & Miniature Golf

While not every child can grow up to be Tiger Woods, everyone can enjoy miniature golf. Full-size golf may be a bit more taxing, but in this area there are many opportunities to try it. See Chapter 5 for details about local golf courses.

Here are some of the best miniature golf locations.

Hidden Valley

Only three and a half miles northwest of Loop 820 on the notorious Jacksboro Highway (see *Gamblers and Gangsters* by Ann Arnold, Eakin Press, 1998), Hidden Valley beckons families. In addition to their golf course, they have a video arcade game room with machines that still take quarters. The use of their picnic area for birthday parties is free of charge (bring your own cake and ice cream) and there are charcoal grills for cooking burgers or hot dogs.

Golf around for $4 per person per game (toddlers get plastic clubs for only $2). A fifty-cent-per-game discount is offered to groups of fifteen or more. After two games, the third is free.

862 I Jacksboro Highway   817-237-5463
Fort Worth, Texas 76135
Hours: Monday-Friday 10 A.M.-10 P.M.
Saturday 10 A.M.-1 1 P.M., Sunday 1 P.M.-10 P.M.
Closed November-March 1

Putt-Putt

Fort Worth   Arlington
7001 Calmont   2004 W. Pleasant Ridge
817-737-2242   817-467-6565

Hurst   Arlington
609 E. Loop 820   1701 E. Division
817-589-0523   817-277-6501

With four locations, Putt-Putt is open year round for golf, games, and batting practice. They have ice cream shops, game rooms, and batting cages at each address. The Hurst and Arlington Division locations feature Go-carts, and there are Bumper Boats at Loop 820.

Golf is $4.95 per game ($1 for kids under six). Multiple game tickets make it a real bargain:

Two games for $6.50, three games for $8.50.
Ten-game family pass (up to ten people) $25.
Birthday party $89.50 for ten children.

Batting Cages and Driving Ranges

See Putt-Putt.

Boating and Water Sports

Considering all the lakes in Texas, there is more shoreline than coastline. Around the Metroplex, it is impossible to travel for more than 30 minutes in any direction without finding water.

The more adventurous can go as far as Austin's Lake Travis for SCUBA diving. Check with the people at Lone Star Scuba for lessons, equipment rental, or purchase and tours.

They often know of or sponsor special low-priced trips to nearby Texas or Caribbean locations and can arrange discounts for groups.

Scuba

Divemasters can lead your underwater adventure to, for example:

Squaw Creek Lake

The Comanche Peak Nuclear Power Station makes the water seem warmer. But it's all in your head. The water doesn't glow in the dark. There are no three-headed fish or sea serpents. SCUBA divers often practice here, and lots of underwater spectacles can be seen. Visibility may be limited after storms, so check the weather when planning a trip.

Lone Star Scuba   817-377-3483
2815 Alta Mere Drive
Fort Worth, Texas 76116

Area Lakes

These watery playgrounds offer opportunities for recreational swimming, boating, fishing, water skiing, and sailing. Check with Parks and Recreation for restrictions and rules. There are far too many to allow complete coverage here, but some of the more notable deserve mention.

In addition to Squaw Creek, lakes in the area include:

Benbrook Lake

Multiple boat ramps at different spots around the perimeter allow for entry of powerboats, jetskis, and sailboats. Great fishing and a swimming beach permit everyone to find some fun. The Army Corps of Engineers keeps this 3,770-acre lake in excellent condition.

There is no fee for use of boat ramps or picnic areas.

Eagle Mountain Lake

This is a 9,200-acre reservoir on the West Fork of the Trinity River. Several marinas around the lake provide launch ramps for a small fee ($7-$10) which includes car and trailer parking. Public ramps sometimes close when the water level is low.

Fishing, water skiing, boating, and sailing are available as are service and recreational facilities, boat rental, and restaurants (see Harbor One, Chapter 20).

Lake Granbury

The Jacob De Cordova Dam on the Brazos River floods 8,700 acres for fishing, water sports, and camping around the 103 miles of shore.

Lake Grapevine

Because this 7,380-acre Corps of Engineers reservoir is home to the Dallas Water Ski Club, it has many competitions and exhibitions in the sport every summer.

Its sixty-mile shoreline is replete with parks and campsites, boat ramps and marinas, picnic areas, and places to sun and swim.

Lake Worth

Follow Meandering Drive, which almost encircles this 3,560-acre site for boating, skiing, and sailing. City parks and picnic areas can be found along the shore along with The Fort Worth Nature Center and Refuge.

Possum Kingdom Lake

Boating, fishing, and SCUBA are a few of the attractions of this 14,440-acre reservoir thirty miles northwest of Mineral Wells. There are numerous resorts and campsites in the environs of the lake.

Joe Pool Lake

Along the Dallas and Tarrant County lines, Joe Pool covers 7,470 acres fed by Mountain Creek. Fishing is excellent, and there are several parks to visit.

Lake Lewisville

The Corps of Engineers built this as Garza-Little Elm Reservoir. The 200-mile shoreline encloses 23,280 acres of recreational water for fishing, boating, skiing, sailing, and camping. More than twenty Corps-run parks can be visited around the lake.

Lake Park, run by the city of Lewisville, is on the south shore. For information call 972-434-1666, or contact City of Lewisville Parks and Leisure Services at 972-219- 3550.

Lake Whitney

Another Corps of Engineers impoundment covering 23,560 acres stretches forty-five miles up the Brazos River near Whitney, Clifton, Meridian, and Hillsboro. With a maximum depth of nearly one hundred feet, it is a paradise for SCUBA divers.

Coves and inlets all around the lake make for excellent fishing. A state record smallmouth bass was caught in 1988.

Parks and marinas, recreation areas, and campsites share lakefront footage with leisure home developments.

Whiterock Lake

Sail in the heart of Dallas. Fishing, boating, and lakeside picnic facilities, but *NO* water skiing.

Ice-skating

Hot, isn't it? The summer of '99 saw temperatures topping 100 degrees for thirty-three days, twenty-four of 'em in a row. Not a record, by any means, but nothing to ignore. How to keep cool without jumping in the pool? Perhaps the answer is a trip to one of the North Texas ice rinks. Ever since Sugarland's Tara Lipinski won Olympic Gold, ice-skating has grown in popularity around here.

The North Texas region boasts an increasing number of ice arenas with attractions ranging from lessons to open skating and facilities for private parties. Practice sessions for the several professional ice hockey teams hereabouts frequently permit public observation.

Skatin' Texas
Cowtown Ice Arena

The Fort Worth Brahmas practice here. Their practices are open, and future hockey Stars or Brahmas may watch. When the Brahmas aren't using the ice, everyone gets to skate. Day care is available on site. Contact Linda Belota for details (817-560-7465).

There's a youth hockey league (Diamond Back), skating lessons, an indoor-outdoor restaurant, and a party room. Late night private rental of the whole place allows for "lock-ins" by school, church, or private groups.

Group discounts can be arranged by calling two days ahead. The party room is available during regular hours.

Birthday parties come in two varieties: Cowtown Cool ($11.50/child, minimum ten) and Texas Terrific ($145 for up to ten children, 14.50 each additional). Both include cake, ice cream, invitations, balloons, paper and plastic supplies, a gift for the birthday child, skating, and skate rental. With "Terrific" they also provide hamburgers, hot dogs, or pizza and a staff "party partner" to help coordinate the event.

3600 Highway 377 South   817-560-RINK (7465)
Fort Worth, Texas 76116-7105   www.skatintexas.com
Hours: Monday 10:45 A.M.-4:45 P.M., Tuesday 10:45 A.M.-3:45 P.M.
Wednesday 10:45 A.M.-5 P.M., Thursday 10:45 A.M.-3:45 P.M.
Friday 10:45 A.M.-4:45 P.M., 7:30-10:30 P.M., Saturday 12:15-3:15 P.M.
Sunday 1-4 P.M.
Rates: $5, Children under five $2
Skate Rental $2
After hours activities:
Lock-ins $800 all night (10:30 P.M.-7 A.M.)
Private ice $200/hour + $1.50 skate rental
Broomball $200/hour
Group Rates: $4.50/person
Day Care: $4.50/child (includes a soda)
Hockey League: ~$500
One game and one practice each week for 20 weeks plus play-offs.

The Ice at Fort Worth Outlet Square

Tired from a long day of shopping the outlet stores at Tandy Center? Cool off in the center of it all and burn some calories. Then replenish them at the eateries encircling the ice.

The rink is open year round and hosts exhibitions and competitions, which are advertised in advance.

Group discounts and lessons are available.

150 Throckmorton Street   817-415-4800
Fort Worth, Texas 76102   817-415-4890
Hours: Monday-Friday 11 A.M.-5:30 P.M., 7:30 P.M.-10 P.M.
Saturday-Sunday 1 P.M.-6 P.M., 7:30 P.M.-10 P.M.
Admission: $4
Skate rental: $1.50
Parking in Fort Worth Outlet Square Garage free for three hours (with validation); or Park Free at Tandy Center lot and ride the subway.

Plaza of the Americas

Another chilling experience is surrounded by a huge office tower/hotel complex with two levels of culinary adventures and several nice shops for gifts, books, candy, and Beanie Babies.

700 North Pearl Street   214-720-8080
Dallas, Texas 75201   www.sk8-edge.com
Skaters Edge of Texas Pro Shop
Hours: Monday-Friday 4:30 P.M.-7:30 P.M., Saturday 9 A.M.-1 P.M.
Closed Sunday

Blue Line Ice Complex

The newest Ice Rink in the area will boast three sheets of ice for skating, hockey, broomball, and parties.

It is also the practice facility for the Texas Tornado Hockey Team, whose practice sessions are open to the public from 3-5 P.M. weekdays. The Tornado plays 60 games between September and April (30 at Blue Line) in the Junior A, Tier 2 amateur league. The arena will seat 2,500 *very* close to the ice. Tickets are $8 and $10. Players are age 20 and under seeking notice by college recruiters. Each team is allowed only two non-U.S. members. Call 817-498-5002 for ticket and schedule information.

Blue Line is still undergoing organizational and scheduling changes, so it is a good idea to call ahead to verify hours and prices.

5208 Airport Freeway   817-788-5400
North Richland Hills, Texas 76117   www.blueline.com
Public skating hours: Monday-Friday 10:15 A.M.-12:15 P.M.
Monday-Sunday 1:30 P.M.-3:30 P.M., Friday-Saturday 7 P.M.-9 P.M.
Admission: $6/2 hours, $2.50 Skate rental
Private lessons available.

Galleria

Like its counterpart in Houston, this is a four-story shopping spree built around a magnificent ice skating rink which, at Christmastime, boasts one of the tallest decorated trees in the country.

Private or group skating lessons can be arranged. Ice skating birthday parties for 10-20 children cost $8.50 per child.

13350 Dallas Parkway   972-392-3361
Dallas, Texas 75240
Hours: Monday 11 A.M.-5 P.M., 8-10 P.M.
Tuesday 11 A.M.-5:30 P.M., 8-10 P.M.
Wednesday 11 A.M.-4:30 P.M., 8-10 P.M.
Thursday 11 A.M.-5 P.M., 8-10 P.M.
Friday 11 A.M.-5 P.M., 6:30-11 P.M.
Saturday noon-11 P.M., Sunday noon-6 P.M.
Admission: Adult $5/ $8 w.skate rental, Senior $4.50
Children 4 and under $3

Bicycling

Because the cityscape has grown so crowded and traffic makes cycling too dangerous, this is a pastime in danger of extinction. Lest the bicycle go the way of the dodo and the passenger pigeon, remember it can be a family activity.

There are several nice trails from which to choose. Most allow access at no charge, although state parks may require admission fees. It is wise to keep in mind that some of these can be crowded on holidays or weekends, so a day off mid-week may be the best time to plan an excursion.

Trinity Park

With more than fifteen miles of paths meandering through the riverside environs and extending away towards other parts of the city, this is the most extensive collection of "rideways" in the region. If you leave the car at Trinity Park, be sure to plan where and when to turn back so no one gets too tired to pedal. And bring water and snacks, if you want them, because they may be hard to find along the way.

River Park

Just north of Bellaire Drive near Lockheed Martin Recreational Area, there is a small parking lot off Bryant Irvin Road. You enter a trail along the Clear Fork of the Trinity River that is mostly level and about three miles long. Its western end crosses a small dam with a nice view of the river. If you still feel energetic, come out and ride on Bellaire Drive through Meadows West and Country Day Estates in lanes marked for bicycles only.

River Legacy Parks

This is another section of the Trinity with five miles of trails winding through woodland, some paved, some not. May be very busy on Sunday afternoons.

Big Bear Creek Greenbelt

A three-and-a-half-mile trail for rides from Bear Creek Park through Keller Sports Park to the Keller-Smithfield activity area. Parking and water fountains at each.

Bear Creek Park   817-431-6044
Keller, Texas

Joe Pool Lake Overlook

A flat path, crossing the top of the dam for four and one half miles. Access and parking is at the eastern approach to the dam. The hours are 6 A.M.-10 P.M.

Cedar Hill Trail

A challenging twelve-and-one-half-mile trail on the east bank of Joe Pool Lake. Better for those with mountain biking experience.

Beginners may prefer to use the hiking trails or ride on the lightly traveled paved roads in the park.

Cedar Hill State Park   972-291-3900
Admission: $5, Children 12 and under free

Lake Mineral Wells State Trailway

This twenty-two-mile trail was converted from a railroad trackbed in the Rails to Trails program. It runs from Mineral Wells State Park to Weatherford through the open country-side and has bridges, wildlife, and police patrols for safety. Hikers and riders (of bicycles and horses) may use it. Trail etiquette requires cyclists to give the right of way to hikers; both must yield to horses.

Access is from either terminus. Cartwright Park in Weather-ford is the southern point of entry. Parking and restrooms can be found at both extremes.

Mineral Wells State Park   940-328-1171
Park admission: Adults (13 and over) $3, Seniors $1
Children under 13 and persons born before 1930 free
Trail admission: Adults $2, Children $1

Roller Skating

This is another activity with numerous locations for partici-pation by all ages. Skates can be in-line or standard (with wheels at each corner).

All locations have party facilities, snack bars, and the availability of lessons.

Check out:

Arlington Skatium	Crowley Road Skate
5515 S. Cooper	10132 Crowley Road
817-784-6222	817-293-2522
Rollerland West	Silver Wheel
7325 Calmont Street	7628 Corina Drive
817-244-8290	817-246-9094

Mountasia Inline Hockey League

Middle and high school competition leagues for the future generation of ice hockey stars. Located at Mountasia Family Fun Center, this is for the sport skaters who are serious about it.

8855 Grapevine Highway	817-788-1051
Fort Worth, Texas 76180	FAX: 817-788-1052

Bowling

Before Don Carter got interested in basketball, he made his fortune renting bowling shoes. Don Carter's All Star Lanes has two locations, one in Dallas and one in Tarrant County. Except during hours restricted to league play, anyone who is able to lift and roll a six-pound ball can enjoy this sport.

For extra-special surroundings, try Showplace Lanes in Euless, where fine dining is available in addition to the usual snacks and drinks.

Don Carter's All Star Lanes Southwest

Locals will remember Don Carter as the former owner of the Dallas Mavericks. Although he is no longer associated with the basketball team, he still has a hand in the bowling game.

Active league play at both All Star locations keeps them full, but there is open bowling every day for those who arrive earliest. Youth leagues admit ages 3-21. Leagues allow keglers of any age above three, but once a youngster is no longer a full-time student he or she must compete in the adult classifications.

Join the birthday club and receive two free games during your birthday month.

6100 Oakmont Boulevard   817-346-0444
Fort Worth, Texas 76132
Fees: Weekends and evenings $3.79
Monday-Friday 9 A.M.-5 P.M.
Adults $2.93/game, Children under 13 $2.35/game
After 5 P.M. and weekends
Adults $3.52/game, Children $2.98/game
Sunday special:
9 A.M.-11 A.M. $14.10/lane (up to 5 bowlers)
11 A.M.-1 P.M. $16.25/lane
After 1 P.M. $19.95/hour or $34.65/two hours
Second location in Dallas:
Don Carter's All Star Lanes West   214-358-1382
10920 Composite
Dallas, Texas 75220
Fees: Monday-Friday 9 A.M.-5 P.M.
Adults $2.71, Children $2.16

Showplace Lanes

With fifty-two lanes open twenty-four hours a day, this is one of the largest bowling alleys in the area. Although much of the time is devoted to league play, there is open bowling every day on a first-come, first-served basis.

Youth leagues start the kids at three years of age with six-pound balls. Once they reach age twenty-one, they must bowl with the grown-ups.

1901 Airport West Freeway   817-283-7144
Euless, Texas 76040
Hours: All Day, Every Day!
Fees: Adults $3.80/Game, Children 17 and under $3.25/Game
Shoe rental $2.00

Shooting/Archery

Indoor and outdoor ranges allow ample opportunity for practice and education about firearms and the bow and arrow.

Arlington Bowhunting World

Ken Witt runs a fully licensed archery pro shop and indoor range. Lessons are offered when bowhunting season is over (January). There are no age restrictions, but an adult must supervise children under eighteen.

6700 W Poly Webb Road   817-478-5990
Arlington, Texas 76016   Metro 817-572-3119
Hours: Tuesday-Friday noon-9 P.M., Saturday 10 A.M.-6 P.M.
Closed Sunday and Monday
Range Fee $6/person

Cowtown Bowmen Archery Club

Young Robin Hoods and Maids Marion can hone their skills in this club with 24-hour daily member access.

8251 Heron Drive   817-367-8696
Fort Worth, Texas 76108
Membership: $25/month
Daily fee: $5

Smithfield Archery and Outdoor Sports

Sam McClasky's full-service archery pro shop has a range for practice and competition that allows children as young as three years of age to shoot (with adult parent supervision).

6616-A Davis Boulevard   817-581-9400
Fort Worth, Texas 76180
Hours: Tuesday-Friday noon-9 P.M., Saturday 9 A.M.-6 P.M.
Fees: $5/hour, $2.50/half-hour, $25/month

Alpine Range

Pistol, rifle, shotgun, and archery! Skeet and trap shooting and a 3-D archery range add to the action.

With a meeting room for group functions, a full-service store for guns and accessories, a kennel (at $4/night, the lowest-priced boarding facility in the area), and instruction available for novice and expert alike, you might never have to leave once you find this place.

How to get there: Take I-20 to Forest Hill Drive (Exit 440) or Anglin Drive (Exit 441). Go south 2 ½ miles. Follow Alpine signs. Or take I-35 south from Fort Worth to Everman Parkway. Go east 2 ½ miles (Everman becomes Shelby Road at first stop sign) and follow signs to Alpine Shooting Range.

5482 Shelby Road   817-478-6613
Fort Worth, Texas 76140   Metro 817-572-1242
Hours: Winter (Standard Time) 8 A.M.-6 P.M.
Summer (Daylight Savings Time) 8 A.M.-7 P.M.
Closed Christmas Day and after noon on Thanksgiving Day
Admission Fee: $6.38

On Target Firearms Training Academy

Located seven miles south of I-20 is another place to learn proper gun etiquette and hone the sharpshooter's eye. With complete firearms sales and service as well as instruction in handgun and long gun usage, including the CHL (concealed handgun license) course, On Target educates shooters and has indoor ranges for handgun and rifle target practice.

14485 Highway 377-S   817-443-1488
Fort Worth, Texas 76126   www.~OTFTAI@flash.net
Hours: Tuesday-Sunday 10 A.M.-9 P.M., Monday noon-8 P.M.
Admission: Handgun range $9.50/hr/lane, Handgun rental $17.50/hr
Rifle range $10/shooter/hr

Soccer

The most popular spectator sport in the world is a favorite for adults as well as children. It is, according to the Fort Worth Youth Soccer Association, the fastest growing sport in the United States and ranks second in youth participation. Tarrant County has active teams in all age categories.

Area clubs and soccer associations are open for membership to players from preschool to adult.

Fort Worth Youth Soccer Association

With teams for players grouped by ages from under six to under nineteen, this organization operates ten privately maintained fields at three locations in Benbrook, West Fort Worth, and South Fort Worth. A fall season holds weekly matches from mid-September to mid-November; spring games take place in late February, March, and April. Each season is followed by a tournament.

P.O. Box 122294
Fort Worth, Texas 76121
817-244-0020
FAX: 817-244-0726

West Side Office:
7700 Calmont (between Cherry
Lane and Alta Mere)

Fees: Ages 5-7 $55/season, Ages 8-13 $60/season, Ages 14-18 $80/season
$5 discount for additional child in same family.
Financial assistance available.

Arlington Soccer Association

This organization has numerous teams in all age categories. Two seasons (fall and spring) of play each year allow Arlington Independent School District students to play on teams drawn from their own neighborhoods. Private school children are not excluded. They play with the team from the area in which they live.

Recreational teams allow players from ages four to eighteen. The *competition* group starts at age ten.

3630 Pioneer Parkway West, Suite 101
Arlington, Texas 76013
Adult Soccer: 817-795-7197
Office Hours:
Monday, Wednesday, Friday 10 A.M.-2 P.M.
Tuesday, Thursday, Friday 5 P.M.-8 P.M.
Registration fee: $40/recreational player
Competition and tournament play additional.

817-261-0242
www.arlingtonsoccer.net
FAX: 817-548-0778

Among other local soccer organizations, contact the following:

Bedford Euless Soccer Association   817-354-4774
3417 Pembroke Place

Fort Worth United Soccer Club, Inc.   817-462-1301
P.O. Box 11484
4333 Bilglade Road
Fort Worth, Texas 76109

Hurst United Soccer Association   817-282-8680
                                           817-485-5449

Chapter 8

Libraries

If you've gotten this far, you know the value of a book. The Fort Worth Public Library System furnishes the community with free reading material year round. It has fourteen places around the city to sit and read with the kids. Or watch movies. Or listen to stories.

Nearby communities such as Arlington, Benbrook, Burleson, Colleyville, Euless, Grapevine, Hurst, White Settlement, Weatherford, and even Dallas have libraries, too. They are open to the public, but you must reside in the locale—or pay a fee—to borrow books from their library.

The library holds an annual book sale to cull the collection of works that are outdated or worn: books, videos, some CD's, and even records—remember them? Call for information: 871-7703.

Central Library

Fort Worth has had a public library since 1901. Growth was sporadic until 1972, when voters approved a new Central Library. Delays and funding difficulties prevented it from opening until 1978 and then only as an underground facility at the Leonard's Department Store end of the Subway to Tandy Center. Not until 1995 was the surface edifice completed. Its interior is still under construction.

The Library is at Taylor and 3rd Streets, two blocks west and two blocks south of the Courthouse on Bus Routes 1-7, 46, and 48.

The Central Library has its own museum-quality gallery with changing exhibits.

300 Throckmorton Street   817-871-7701
Fort Worth, Texas 76102-7333
http://198.215.16.8:443/fortworth/fwpl
Hours: Sunday noon-6 P.M., Monday-Thursday 9 A.M.-9 P.M.
Friday-Saturday 10 A.M.-6 P.M.

Library Divisions

With two regional libraries, nine branch libraries, and two satellite libraries, the Fort Worth Library System has ample room for readers to gather. A new Summerglen Branch in the planning stages is expected to open in the fall/winter of 2000/2001. The 11,000-square-foot facility at 4205 Basswood Boulevard will serve the communities of Summerfields, Park Glen, and Fossil Creek.

Regional Libraries

Southwest Regional

Located on South Hulen Street, six blocks north of South Loop 820 at Briarhaven Road, the Southwest Regional Library is served by Bus Route 25.

This 25,000-square-foot facility opened in 1987 and circulates almost a million items each year. It hosts a Fort Worth Public Library Reading Club, Preschool Storytime (Thursdays at 10:30 A.M.), a demonstration garden by the Fort Worth Native Plant Society, and Family Movies (Saturdays at 3 P.M.)

4001 Library Lane   817-782-9853
Fort Worth, Texas 76109-4495
Hours: Sunday noon-6 P.M., Tuesday-Thursday 10 A.M.-9 P.M.

Friday-Saturday 10 A.M.-6 P.M.
Closed Monday

East Regional

Located on the north access road to I-30 two blocks west of East Loop 820 at Bridge and Oakland Hills Drive, it is on Bus Route 21.

In addition to the FWPL Reading Club, East Regional has an Adult Learning Center with GED, ESL, literacy and citizenship instruction.

Storytime for ages 3-6 is Thursday at 10 A.M.

6301 Bridge Street   817-871-6436
Fort Worth, Texas 76112-0823
Hours: Sunday noon-6 P.M., Tuesday-Thursday 10 A.M.-9 P.M.
Friday-Saturday 10 A.M.-6 P.M.
Closed Monday

Branch Libraries

These are placed so that each section of the city has access to books and other printed and audio/visual material.

Diamond Hill/Jarvis

This small branch opened in 1989. It is at 35th and Decatur on Bus Route 28. Besides holding a bilingual storytime every Saturday afternoon at 2, it also has a GED, ESL, and citizenship learning center open Monday and Wednesday evenings from 5-9 P.M. Computer-assisted/subject tutoring is held Monday, Wednesday 5-8 P.M., and Saturday 10 A.M.-4 P.M.

1300 N.E. 35th Street   817-624-7331
Fort Worth, Texas 76106-4552
Hours: Monday, Wednesday noon-9 P.M.
Tuesday, Thursday, Saturday 10 A.M.-6 P.M.
Closed Sunday

East Berry

This 9,250-square-foot branch has been serving the area since 1967. It is at the intersection of E. Berry and Griggs on

Bus Routes 24, 25, and in Rider Request Area 42 (call 817-215-8600 for a reservation).

Storytime is at 10:30 A.M. on Tuesday. The branch also offers a youth intervention program called SOUL (Services and Opportunities United by the Library) for ages 12-21. Weekly programs take place Wednesday and Thursday 4-6 P.M. Call for more information.

4300 E. Berry   817-536-1945
Fort Worth, Texas 76105-5003
Hours: Tuesday, Friday, Saturday 10 A.M.-6 P.M.
Wednesday-Thursday noon-9 P.M.
Closed Sunday, Monday

Meadowbrook

The 5,664-square-foot building at E. Lancaster and Stark opened in 1964 to provide this section of town with library services. It is five blocks west of East Loop 820 on Bus Routes 2, 21, 22, and 25 (transfers at Eastside Transfer Center).

Storytime is Friday at 10:30 A.M.

The GED Learning Center is open Tuesday and Wednesday, 5-9 P.M. The branch has a special collection of Vietnamese books, videos, and audio recordings.

5651 East Lancaster   817-451-0916
Fort Worth, Texas 76112-6430
Hours: Tuesday, Wednesday noon-9 P.M.
Thursday, Friday, Saturday 10 A.M.-6 P.M.
Closed Sunday, Monday

Northside

Opened: 1967. Size: 7,575 square feet. Location: five blocks west of intersection of North Main and 20th Street.

Bus Route 1 and Rider Request Area 48 (call 817-215-8600 for reservation).

Storytime: Saturday 2 P.M. (ages four and up).

This branch also has a GED and ESL Learning Center, a Spanish book section, and a Hispanic Heritage Collection.

Special attractions include the Jalapeno Players, a young adult program about puppetry; Crafts with Mr. Pete, Thursdays at 6:30 P.M.; and computer-assisted/subject tutoring on Tuesday and Thursday 5:30-8:30 P.M., and Saturday 10 A.M.-6 P.M.

LATINO (Library Assisting The Individuals Needing Our Support), a gang prevention program for youths 8-14 provides an after-school resource center Tuesday, Thursday 3-8 P.M., Wednesday, Friday 3-6 P.M., and Saturday 10 A.M.-6 P.M.

601 Park   817-626-8241
Fort Worth, Texas 76106-8096
Hours: Tuesday-Thursday noon-9 P.M.
Wednesday, Friday, Saturday 10 A.M.-6 P.M.
Closed Sunday, Monday

Ridglea

Opened: 1967. Size: 10,754 square feet.

Ridglea Avenue continues south of Camp Bowie Boulevard as Bernie Anderson. The library is just northwest of the entrance to Ridglea Country Club. It is on Bus Route 2.

Preschool Storytime is Friday at 11 A.M.

There is also a GED and ESL Learning Center and an Avid Readers Club, which meets at 2 P.M. on the second Friday of each month.

3628 Bernie Anderson   817-737-6619
Fort Worth, Texas 76116-5403
Hours: Tuesday-Wednesday noon-9 P.M.
Thursday, Friday, Saturday 10 A.M.-6 P.M.
Closed Sunday, Monday

Riverside

Nine blocks east of I-35W at Chandler on Bus Route 3, this 8,197-square-foot branch opened in 1967. It features books and videos in both Spanish and Vietnamese and a GED

Learning Center open from 5-9 P.M. on Wednesday and Thursday.

Preschool Storytime is Tuesday at 10 A.M.

2913 Yucca Drive   817-838-6931
Fort Worth, Texas 76111-4351
Hours: Tuesday, Friday, Saturday 10 A.M.-6 P.M.
Wednesday, Thursday noon-9 P.M.
Closed Sunday, Monday

Seminary South

Another branch that has been around since 1967, with 7,741 square feet of literary space, it is one block north and one block west of the intersection of I-35W and Seminary Drive on Bus Routes 1 and 25. It is in Rider Request Area 43 (call 817-215-8600 for reservations).

The branch carries an African/American collection as well as books and videos in Spanish.

Preschool Storytime is Saturday at 10:30 A.M.

501 E. Bolt   817-926-0215
Fort Worth, Texas 76110-6310
Hours: Monday, Tuesday, Saturday 10 A.M.-6 P.M.
Wednesday, Thursday noon-9 P.M.
Closed Friday, Sunday

Shamblee

Opened in 1982 in the Southside Community Center, this is a small branch (only 2,956-square feet), but it has a good collection of works on African/American heritage and African/American fiction as well as Spanish books and videos.

It is five blocks east of I-35W at New York Avenue on Bus Route 4.

Storytime for ages 3-5 is Tuesday at 11:30 A.M.

Reading and math tutoring for grades 1-8 is available Monday 4-6 P.M. and Tuesday 5:30-7:30 P.M.

959 E. Rosedale   817-871-6621

Fort Worth, Texas 76104-5195
Hours: Monday, Tuesday 11 A.M.-8 P.M.
Wednesday-Friday 10 A.M.-6 P.M.
Closed Saturday, Sunday

Wedgwood

Two blocks south of SW Loop 820 in Rider Request Area 44 (817-215-8600). This one opened with 5,664 square feet of book space in 1962.

Storytime is Wednesday and Thursday at 10:30 A.M.

3816 Kimberly Drive   817-292-3368
Fort Worth, Texas 76133-2021
Hours: Monday, Tuesday noon-9 P.M.
Wednesday, Thursday, Saturday 10 A.M.-6 P.M.
Closed Friday, Sunday

Satellite Libraries

Fort Worth has two of these located in Public Housing Developments.

COOL: Cavile Outreach Opportunity Library

This was opened in 1994 in a one-story, 915-square-foot apartment in the Cavile Public Housing Community. It is on Bus Routes 4 and 25, six blocks west of E Loop 820 from the Rosedale exit and one block south on Etta.

Preschool Storytime is Wednesday at 3 P.M.

5060 Avenue G   817-534-0852
Fort Worth, Texas 76105-1906
Hours: Tuesday, Thursday 11 A.M.-8 P.M.
Wednesday, Friday, Saturday 11 A.M.-6 P.M.
Closed Sunday, Monday

BOLD: Butler Outreach Library Division

BOLD is located in the Butler Housing Community, which is bordered by I35W on the west, I30 on the south, and U.S. 287 on the east. Access from the south is via Lancaster, north on Pine (it becomes Cypress after crossing I30), around the former I. M. Terrell High School, right on Luella, and left on Stevenson for one block. It is on Bus Route 9.

It opened in 1997, has 1,400-square feet, and its special collections include reference materials to support homework assignments plus a selection of sought-after reading material, including children's and self-help titles. They also have popular periodicals and African-American materials.

Storytime is Saturdays at 3, for ages 3-12.

1801 N/S Freeway   817-338-1467
Fort Worth, Texas 76102-5742
Hours: Tuesday, Thursday 11 A.M.-8 P.M.
Wednesday, Friday, Saturday 11 A.M.-6 P.M.
Closed Sunday, Monday

Community Libraries

Libraries in other nearby towns offer similar amenities. Readers need never go wanting. Storytime is popular at many of these:

Arlington
Central Branch
101 E. Abram   817-459-6900/6907
Storytime: Tuesday 10, 11 A.M. (age 2)
        Wednesday 9:15, 10:15, 11:15 A.M. (age 3-7)
        Thursday 6:30 P.M. (2-3), 7 P.M. (4-7)
        Friday 10:30 A.M. (under 2)
Northeast
1905 E. Brown Blvd.   817-277-5573
Storytime: Tuesday, Wednesday 10:30 A.M. (3-7), 11:15A.M. (age 2)
        Wednesday 7 P.M. (under 2)
        Thursday 7 P.M. (age 2-3)
East
1624 New York Ave.   817—275-3321
Storytime: Thursday 10:15 A.M. (age 3-7), 11:15 A.M. (age 2)
Southwest
4000 Green Oaks Blvd.   817-478-3762
Storytime: Monday 10:15, 10:45 A.M. (age 2)
        Wednesday, Thursday 10:15 A.M. (3-7)

Woodland West
2837 W. Park Row   817-277-5265
Storytime: Tuesday 10:30 A.M. (age 3-7), 11:15 A.M. (age 2)

Bedford
3601 W. Pipeline Road   817-952-2160/2451
Storytime: Reading Circle Monday 4-5 P.M. (grades K-2)
            Tuesday, Wednesday 10 A.M. (age 2-3, with adult)
            11 A.M. (age 3-5)

Burleson
248 SW Johnson Ave.   817-295-6131
Storytime and Puppet Theater:
            Tuesday 10:30 A.M. (toddlers)
            Wednesday 10:30 A.M. (age 3 and up)

Hurst
901 Precinct Line Road   817-788-7300
Storytime: Wednesday, Friday 10:45 A.M. (age 3-Kindergarten)
            Thursday 10 A.M. (12 Mos.-36 Mos.)

Keller
640 Johnson Road   817-431-9011
Storytime: Tuesday, Wednesday 10 A.M. and 11:15 (18 Mos.-36 Mos.)
            10:30 A.M. (age 3-6)
            Tuesday 2 P.M. (age 3-6), 1:15 P.M. (Home schoolers)

Lake Worth
3801 Adams Grub Drive   817-237-9681
Storytime: Thursday 10 A.M. (age 3-5)

Roanoke
201 Main Street   817-491-2691
Storytime: Friday, Saturday 10:30 A.M.

White Settlement
214 Meadow Park Drive   817-367-0166
Storytime: Tuesday 9:45 A.M. (age 3 ½-6)

Other

Storytime is also held at the following Barnes and Noble bookstores:

Grapevine   817-251-1997
　　Tuesday 10:30 A.M. (all ages)
　　Friday 7 P.M. (under 9), 7:45 P.M. (9 and up)

North Arlington   817-277-5184
　　Monday 10 A.M.

North Richland Hills   817-281-7042
　　Wednesday, Saturday 11 A.M.

South Arlington   817-557-1171
　　Wednesday, Saturday 11 A.M.
　　Sundance Square (817-332-7178)
　　Friday 7 P.M.

University Park   817-335-2791
　　Tuesday 11 A.M.
　　Friday 7 P.M.

Chapter 9

Special Attractions

These are wild wonderlands, home of the weird, the wet, and the wacky. Spend a few hours or a couple of days. New discoveries await you around every corner.

Six Flags Over Texas

One of twenty-five Premiere Parks around the United States, Arlington's Six Flags Over Texas is home to the Texas Giant. The tallest wooden roller coaster in the world will carry anyone who is at least 48 inches tall on a two-minute breathtaking ride. If this were the only thing to do at Six Flags, it would still be an exciting place to visit. There are, however, many other activities.

Thrilling rides vie with shows like Illusionaria, Gotham City Carnival of Chaos, and the Texas Backlot gunfighters. Frequent concerts showcase international singing sensations; season ticket holders get free admission on performance day.

Special activities for the kids include Looney Tunes Land, Silver Star Carousel, Air Racer, the Mini Mine Train, and Splash Water. Need more excitement? Try the Viper (*La Vibora*) or Yosemite Sam's Gold River Adventure, and try to help Sheriff Bugs Bunny find the thief. Or ride El Sombrero, the whirling Mexican hat.

2201 Road to Six Flags
Arlington, Texas 76010

817-640-8900
www.sixflags.com

Hours: Seasonal variation, call or check website
Summer hours from Memorial Day Weekend to the end of July 10 A.M.-10 P.M.
Admission: Adult $37.99, Adult 2-days (consecutive) $41.99
Children under four feet tall and Seniors $18.99/2-days $37.99
Parking $8
Children under 2 years Free
Season Pass $69.99/four or more $54.99 ea.
Season Parking pass $30/Each additional $10
All prices plus tax

If the Gold River Adventure doesn't get you wet enough, travel a short distance east on I-30 to the other Metroplex Six Flags attraction:

Hurricane Harbor

From Hook's Lagoon to Boogie Beach, everyone gets wet at Hurricane Harbor. Newly opened in 1999, Hook's Lagoon is a five-story interactive water playground with climbing nets and water slides and a 1,000-gallon bucket suspended above that tips every so often to ensure a saturated experience.

Along Boogie Beach, twenty-four thousand gallons of rushing water per minute create a spectacular wave. Hang ten!

Shops like Cabana Brothers and Hook's Treasures sell bathing suits, beach clothes, accessories, toys, and gifts.

How to get there: From Dallas or Fort Worth take IH-30 to Arlington. Exit at Ballpark Way. Go north to Lamar Boulevard and turn left. Watch for signs. Consider using Highway 360 and exit at Brown Boulevard. Go west on Brown to Ballpark Way. Go south (left) to second light (Lamar). Turn right and go two blocks. Hurricane Harbor is on left.

1800 E. Lamar Boulevard   817-265-3356
Arlington, Texas 76006
www.sixflags.com/hurricaneharbordallas/
Admission: Adults $24.99, seniors over 55 and children $12.50
Children 2 and under free

Parking $5
Season Pass $69.99
All prices plus tax

Ripley's Believe It Or Not/Wax Museum

Just down the road from Six Flags and Hurricane Harbor, in a building reminiscent of the Taj Mahal, the Palace of Wax shares space with Ripley's—believe it or not!

Check out the truly bizarre and take a trek through history with figures so lifelike, you'll expect them to speak.

At the end of the Palace of Wax tour is the Museum of Fear, a horrible area where killers lurk. Each year as all Hallows Eve (Halloween) approaches, this section becomes a haunted house called "Singe." It may be a little severe for young children, but the teens will tolerate it with ease.

How to get there: From Dallas or Fort Worth take IH-30 to Grand Prairie. Exit north at Beltline Road.

601 E. Safari Parkway   972-263-2391
Grand Prairie, Texas 75050   www.ripleys.com
E-mail: timb@classicattractions.com
Hours:
Memorial Day-Labor Day 10 A.M.-9 P.M.
September-October 7
Monday-Friday 10 A.M.-5 P.M., Saturday-Sunday 10 A.M.-6 P.M.
October 8-May
Monday-Thursday 10 A.M.-5 P.M., Friday-Saturday 10 A.M.-4 P.M.
Sunday 10 A.M.-6 P.M.
Admission: Adults $10.95/$14.95, Children 4-12 $6.95/$9.95
Seniors $9.95, Groups of 12 or more $8.95 each
Combination discount tickets to both attractions available.
"Singe" Halloween at the Wax Museum
Admission: Adults $15, Children under 13 $11
Hours: Fridays and Saturdays in October 7 P.M.-midnight
October 31 6 P.M.-10 P.M.

NRH2O

The name says it all: the family water park in North Richland Hills. Jump in the 12,000-square-foot NRH2Ocean and swim, surf, or come on Friday night for the "Dive In" movies. Lots of lounge chairs let the parents relax on the NRH2Ocean beach while they watch the kids splash in the waves.

The Endless River flows through landscaped sections of the park, giving everyone a casual summer float trip. Tubes are free. Professor Frogstein's Forest, near the Ocean, has picnic tables and is an ideal place for group functions.

Four different water slides allow every age group the chance to slip and swirl. The Double Dipper features two-person tubes.

Tad Pole Train Station for kids 54" or shorter is a full-size train loaded with interactive activities to sustain saturation.

The ultimate experience is The Green Extreme. This is the world's largest *uphill* water coaster. Two riders per boat travel seven stories high through 1,161 feet of twisting, diving, and looping tunnels at 19 feet per second.

The park is available for private rental. The Covered Pavilion and Forest Picnic Area can be reserved for all-day use. Contact the Group Sales Office (817-656-6500) for details.

How to get there: From Dallas take Highway 183 west to Precinct Line Road. Go north to Highway 26 (Grapevine Highway). Turn left. NRH2O will be on the right. You also reach Highway 26 by continuing on 183. If coming from Fort Worth, take Loop 820 north or east to Highway 26 and go north. NRH2O will be on the left across from the Northeast Campus of Tarrant Community College.

900 Grapevine Highway
North Richland Hills, Texas 76180
Hours: Seasonal, call.

817-656-6500
FAX: 817-656-6530
www.nrh2o.com

Summer hours: Mid-June through first week in August
Sunday-Thursday 10 A.M.-8 P.M., Friday-Saturday 10 A.M.-10 P.M.
Admission: 54" and taller $12.95, Under 54" $10.95
Age 2 and under free, Groups of 15 or more $9.95 each
(Must have one adult for every six children under age 6.)
Discounts:

Group size	Prepaid price	Prereserved price
15-50	$9.25	$9.50
51-125	$8.75	$9.00
126-350	$8.25	$8.50
351-600	$7.50	$8.00
601-1000	$7.00	$7.50
1000-3000	$6.50	$7.00

Season Passes:
One $79.95, Two $149.90, Three $194.85, Four $229.80

Mountasia Family Fun Center

Here's one more amusement complex with activities for all ages. Go-carts, skating, miniature golf, skill and water games keep visitors from boredom. Bumper boats are floating fun for anyone—driver must be 44" tall; passengers 36"-54" and drivers with passengers must be at least 13 years old.

Batting cages enable the next generation of sluggers to prepare a challenge to "The Babe's" record (or Mark McGuire's or Sammy Sosa's). Twenty pitches for $1 served up to anyone at least 48" tall.

Snacks, souvenirs, and gifts fill tummies and memories. The facility is available for lock-ins, birthday parties, and corporate outings.

8851 Grapevine Highway   Metro 817-498-4488
Fort Worth, Texas 76180   817-788-0990
Hours: Winter, Fall and Spring   FAX: 817-788-9740
Sunday-Thursday noon-10 P.M., Friday noon-midnight
Saturday 10 A.M.-midnight
Summer Monday-Thursday 10 A.M.-11 P.M.
Friday-Saturday 10-midnight, Sunday noon-10 P.M.

Chapter 10

Military Installations and Industry

Military Installations

Fort Worth has a long and distinguished military history stretching back to the days when Major Ripley Arnold commanded the fort that became the nucleus of the city. Arnold served in the Army of the Southwest under Major General William Jenkins Worth, who led the Eighth and Ninth Divisions (Texas and New Mexico) and never set foot in Fort Worth. He was, in fact, a native of New York, who gained distinction in the conflict with the Seminoles in Florida, where he and Arnold met.

The connection between Fort Worth and the military was further strengthened in the early years of the twentieth century by the dynamism and foresight of Amon G. Carter. His power and influence as mayor of Fort Worth, along with his position as editor and publisher of the *Fort Worth Star*, enabled him to attract Consolidated Vultee Aircraft Corporation to the city in 1941. The Convair Factory, completed in April 1942, built B-24s and, later, B-32s and B-36s.

"Bomber City," home to many of the aircraft manufacturer's employees, grew into White Settlement. Convair became first General Dynamics, then Lockheed. Subsequent merger with Martin-Marietta finally resulted in the present-day Lockheed-Martin.

The Army, followed by the newly created Air Force, maintained Tarrant Field adjacent to the factory. It was renamed Carswell Air Force Base in February 1948, in memory of Air Force Major Horace S. Carswell, a Fort Worth holder of the Congressional Medal of Honor, who was killed in China.

Those interested in history will find Oliver Knight's *Fort Worth Outpost on the Trinity* (Texas Christian University Press, 1953 and 1990) fascinating reading. The White Settlement Museum and the Vintage Aviation Museum (see Chapters 3 and 4) also have outstanding historical displays, as does the Fort Worth Museum of Science and History.

Carswell/ Joint Reserve Base/ NAS

Tours of the base are arranged through the Public Affairs Office. School and scouting groups frequently visit. A call to 817-782-7815 is the first step. The base is not open to visitors without clearance or prior arrangement.

This is the home of the 301st Fighter Wing, Marine Aircraft Group 41 and Fighter Squadron 201.

How to get there: From downtown take IH-30 west to Highway 183 and go north. Follow General Arnold Drive past Shady Oaks Country Club and go left on Pumphrey Drive to Carswell Access Road.

Industry

There are numerous opportunities to visit business and industrial sites in and around Fort Worth. Some of the potentially most interesting cannot entertain guests due to restrictions imposed by their insurance policies or the Department of Health. One such is O.B. (Our Best) Macaroni Company, a family-owned pasta maker in Fort Worth for over one hundred years. Although you cannot tour the building, they maintain an excellent website that is worth a looksee (www.obpasta.com). O.B. Macaroni Company, located at 108 South Freeway (I-35 W), is the only Italian-owned pasta maker in Texas.

Northrop Grumman Corporation cannot allow small children to tour because of the injury risk in its manufacturing areas. The company's website is an excellent one, however, and substitutes very nicely for visits (see below).

Lockheed-Martin Tactical Aircraft Systems

The builder of the F-16 and its successor, the F-22, is moving into the twenty-first century with new and remarkable aircraft, such as the Joint Strike Fighter and the UCAV (Uninhabited Combat Air Vehicle).

The Fort Worth plant, which started as Convair, is engaged in the development of X-33 VentureStar, the next generation of space shuttles, aircraft capable of taking 25,000 pounds of payload to the orbiting space station and returning to Earth.

Tours of the plant are best arranged on a personal level by contacting an individual employee. Groups with a business or career interest, such as Scout engineering groups or college students, can be sponsored through the Public Affairs section. Most large groups, however, must tour after hours. Regular visiting time is generally at 10 A.M. on weekdays.

Take a preliminary excursion through Lockheed's facilities at the stunning website, featuring aerial views of some of the most amazing aircraft in the world, not to mention an excellent history of aviation.

Lockheed Boulevard   817-777-2000
Fort Worth, Texas   www.lmtas.com

Northrop Grumman Corporation

With major contracts in both military aerospace and commercial aviation, this company is intimately involved in the aircraft production business in the Metroplex. Although headquartered in Los Angeles, Northrop Grumman's Integrated Systems and Aerostructures Sector (ISA) runs significant production facilities in Grand Prairie. They manufacture portions of the Joint Surveillance Target Attack Radar System (Joint STARS) and the B-2 Stealth Bomber. Northrop also builds sections of commercial aircraft, including fuselage and tail sections, doors, control surfaces, and nacelles and thrust reversers.

Visit the website for pictures and information.

9314 West Jefferson Boulevard   972-946-2011
Dallas, Texas 75211-2011   www.northgrum.com

General Motors Arlington Assembly Plant

The Arlington Assembly Plant is currently involved in a major project to enlarge the body shop. Tours are suspended until completion in late 2000. When the construction is completed, they should resume and visitors will be able to see the assembly line for the Chevrolet and GMC pickup trucks, Yukon/Tahoe, and Cadillac Escalade. Call to find out if the tours are running and to schedule visits.

2525 East Abram Street   817-652-2098/2099 (Personnel)
Arlington, Texas 76010   817-652-2541 (Training)
www.gmc.com

Acme Bricks

School, scouting, and family groups interested in learning the finer points of brick making will enjoy a visit to Acme's factory. Acme operates two brick plants in this region. One is west of Weatherford, Texas, and the other is in Denton. To arrange a visit at either one, call Larry Clements (817-390-2409).

2811 West Seventh Street   817-390-2409
Fort Worth, Texas 76107   817-332-4101

Burlington Northern and Santa Fe RR

This transportation giant's Fort Worth facility is the Network Operations Center, the computerized heart of its national railroad web. It is open to visits by groups, including school classes and scout troops. There they can see how the trains are kept on schedule and coordinated to deliver people and products all over North America. Call Jerry Jenkins (817-352-6420) to make arrangements.

1-800-289-2673   817-333-2000

Mrs. Baird's Bread

Mrs. Baird's Bread has been around Fort Worth since 1908, when Ninnie L. Baird, a young widow, sold home-baked bread to friends and neighbors. Ninety years later, the Baird family is still involved in the baking of bread, pies, and cakes for the neighbors. The neighborhood, as Vernon Baird once said, "has gotten a little bigger."

The recent purchase by Grupo Bimbo, a Mexican baking company with a similar family history, made Mrs. Baird's an international company.

Tours of the modern, computerized bakery are held Monday, Wednesday, and Friday by appointment. Call or e-mail Linda Medina (817-293-6230 Lmedina@mrsbairds.com) to make the arrangements. Children must be at least six years old to visit.

7301 South Freeway   817-293-6230
Fort Worth, Texas 6134   www.mrsbairds.com

Star-Telegram

Fort Worth's hometown newspaper has a program of tours of the printing plant. Those interested in going behind the scenes at the Star-Telegram will see the inner workings of the presses along with robot paper carriers. Call Haskell Dotson (817-215-2240) to make the arrangements. Tours start at 10 A.M. Monday-Friday, for groups of ten to thirty-five.

While there, you can also see the longhorns grazing in the pasture south of the plant. Rusty headlines the group. He is a Grand Champion Steer purchased by the newspaper from the Stock Show. His stock market picking has become well known in local competition with the experts, and that's "no bull."

400 West Seventh Street
Fort Worth, Texas 76102
817-390-7400
www.star-telegram.com

Printing Plant
685 John B. Sias
Fort Worth, Texas 76132
817-215-2240

Vending Nut Company

Call Jack Ellis to arrange a visit and learn how nuts are roasted. This is a quick stop a few blocks from the Museum of Science and History, so it would be possible to combine the tour and a visit to the museum in the same day.

2222 Montgomery Street
Fort Worth, Texas 76107

817-737-3071

The Studios at Las Colinas

With more than 100,000 annual visitors to the Studios at Las Colinas Tour, they must be doing something right. This facility is the largest motion picture production complex between Florida and California, prompting the nickname "The Third Coast." Not only are movies, commercials, and TV programs made here, they also provide complete production of musical, video, or film projects from start to finish for professional or private use.

The National Museum of Communications holds a Guttenburg printing press, early telephone switchboards and radios, and the first color television ever made.

Book the Studios for group tours, parties, or special events (972-869-7752).

Dallas Communications Complex
6301 North O'Connor Road
Building One
Irving, Texas 75039
www.studiosatlascolinas.com

972-869-FILM (3456)
Group Tours or Events:
972-869-7752
1-800-914-0006

Chapter 11

Youth Organizations and Camps

The Fort Worth Camera Club is open to youth and adults, meets twice each month, and has a monthly photography contest for members. Visitors are welcome. Meetings are held at the Texas College of Osteopathic Medicine, North Texas Health Science Center, 3500 Camp Bowie Boulevard, Fort Worth, Medical Education Extension Building 2, Room 2-106, on the first and third Thursdays of each month at 7:30 P.M. Find out more at their website (www.star-tele-gram.com/homes/fwcamclub/).

The Greater Fort Worth Sierra Club convenes on the third Wednesday of each month with a program on ecology or natural history. They also sponsor frequent outings such as hikes, campouts, and backpacking trips. For more information call 817-588-1167 or write P.O. Box 1925, Fort Worth, Texas 76101. Find them on the web at www.sierraclub.org. Monthly meeting is in the Main Auditorium, Texas College of Osteopathic Medicine, North Texas Health Science Center, 3500 Camp Bowie Boulevard, Fort Worth.

Annual membership fees for the different clubs—and there are many others—vary but are quite reasonable.

Other community clubs include these more widely known organizations:

Boy Scouts of America

A charter member of the World Scout Conference, BSA directs scouting activities for all interests and skill levels for boys aged six-eighteen, from Cub to Explorer Scout. Begun in England in 1907 based on the formulas set down by Robert S. S. Baden-Powell in his book *Scouting for Boys*, this has become the largest voluntary youth movement in the world. The Longhorn Council directs about 250 Boy Scout Troops and many Cub Packs in the eleven counties around Fort Worth. When the Cub Scouts hold their annual Pinewood Derby, April 15, 2000, *everyone* (including parents) is welcome to compete.

Specialized Explorer groups highlighting interests in occupations such as medicine or law enforcement give high school students a foretaste of their chosen career paths.

Longhorn Council
4917 Briarhaven Road
Fort Worth, Texas 76109
www.startext.net/homes/longhorn

817-738-5491
www.longhorn.org
www.bsa.scouting.org

Girl Scouts Inc.

The Circle T Girl Scout Council oversees scouting in Tarrant, Hood, Johnson, and Somervell Counties. Girl Scouting began in Georgia in 1912 when Juliette Gordon Low organized the first troop in Savannah. Thirty years later, the first Fort Worth Council was chartered. Now, the Circle T Council boasts nearly 15,000 girl and 5,000 adult members.

Their facilities include Morrison Lodge in Haltom City, two Girl Scout Houses in Arlington, Camp Timberlake on Eagle Mountain Lake, and Stevens Ranch on the Brazos River near Glen Rose. They also manage the Girl Scout Service Centers in Fort Worth, Arlington, and North Richland Hills.

4901 Briarhaven Road   817-737-7272
Fort Worth, Texas 76109   www.circletgsc.org

Campfire Boys and Girls

Founded in Fort Worth in 1914 as an organization for young girls, Campfire became co-educational in 1976 and has, since then, offered club and activity programs for boys and girls from five to eighteen years of age. Membership now approaches twenty-five thousand. Nine thousand adult volunteers and almost twenty thousand child-care providers ensure no enrolled child is ignored. A series of special activities and community services are aimed to help the "at risk" segment of the juvenile population with after-school and summer day-camp programs to foster responsible attitudes and develop healthy minds and bodies.

Campfire operates Camp *El Tesoro* (the Treasure) near Granbury, Texas. This scenic locale hosts summer camp sessions and *El Tesoro de la Vida* (the Treasure of Life), a weeklong resident healing experience for bereaved children. In addition, there are numerous area day-camp sites for children aged five to twelve years.

First Texas Council   817-831-2111
2700 Meacham Boulevard   www.firsttexascampfire.org
Fort Worth, Texas 76137

Boys and Girls Clubs of Greater Fort Worth

A place for youth on the edge to stay on the right side with support from dedicated professionals and volunteers and the help of law enforcement authorities.

Boys and Girls Clubs involve young people in educational and community service projects. For example, one project allows former gang members in the "Comin' Up" program to have tattoos removed in exchange for community service (painting out graffiti around the city is one popular form).

3218 East Belknap Street   817-834-4711
Fort Worth, Texas 76111-4739   www.bgcfortworth.org
E-mail: bgc@startext.net

Big Brothers and Big Sisters

Big Brothers and Sisters serve as mentors for youngsters in single-parent homes and to those who might be at risk in other ways. Big Siblings accompany these kids after school, take them to work, or just "hang" with them to talk and act as a good role model. Volunteers are always welcome.

Big Brothers and Big Sisters of Fort Worth, Inc.

901 Summit Avenue   817-654-0155
Fort Worth, Texas 76102   817-877-4277
www.bbbsa.org

Big Brothers and Big Sisters of Arlington, Inc.

205 West Main Street   817-265-4777
Arlington, Texas 76010   817-277-1148

YMCA

The YMCA runs fifteen centers in Fort Worth and another four in Arlington. Families can engage in swimming and other athletic pastimes as well as crafts. After-school custodial care is also provided.

YWCA has several sites in Fort Worth for residential and day care services. The downtown YWCA has an excellent ballroom and party facility that can be rented for private and corporate functions.

Indian Guides and Indian Princesses are scouting-type activities offered under the administrative umbrella of the "Y"-organization.

817-335-9622	**Fort Worth YMCA**
Indian Guides	817-335-9622
Indian Princesses	
Arlington YMCA	**YWCA**
220 South Davis	512 West 4th Street
Arlington, Texas 76013	Fort Worth, Texas 76102
817-274-9622	817-332-67191

Young Life

A nondenominational Christian organization that holds weekly supervised meetings at which high school kids can be boisterous yet remain under control. Also sponsors summer sleep-away camps. Young Life promotes wholesome lifestyles and reliable behavior.

2501 Forest Park Boulevard	817-926-5441
Fort Worth, Texas 76110	www.younglife.org

B'Nai B'Rith Youth Organization

B'Nai B'Rith Youth Organization is similar in its goals to Young Life. It maintains two active groups in Fort Worth, one for girls 14-18 (BBG Alton-Silver) and one for boys in the same age range (BBB Rubin-Gilbert). The headquarters for the region is in Dallas.

7900 Northaven Road	**B'Nai B'Rith Fort Worth**
Dallas, Texas 75230	5280 Trail Lake Drive
214-363-4654	Fort Worth, Texas 76133
	817-346-4493

Chapter 12

Tours

Touring can be around the neighborhood, around the city, around the Metroplex, or off into the wild blue yonder.

One nice thing about Fort Worth is its relative compactness. Walking tours won't tire you if you do them one section at a time. Start in downtown and see the Courthouse, Bass Performance Hall, Sundance Square, the Convention Center, and the Water Gardens. You'll still have time for lunch and a visit to The Ice at Tandy Center. And you won't get exhausted. Even the little ones can keep up.

An entire day should be saved for the Stockyards and another for the Zoo or the Botanic Gardens (see Chapters 5 and 6). If you have more time, plan a trip to one of the many interesting nearby communities (Granbury, Glen Rose, Weatherford, Waco, or, perhaps, Austin—the state capital). Perhaps Dallas, too, if you're a glutton for punishment.

A day in Merrie Olde England can be had during the spring session of Scarborough Faire near Waxahachie (see Chapter 17). Guided tours may be preferred if you can keep to a schedule.

Gray Line Tours

Gray Line runs numerous bus tours to the local sights in and around the Metroplex. Many operate on a scheduled basis, picking up and dropping off at several Dallas locations.

119

Charter bus service is another part of their business, so when the family gets big enough contact Gray Line!

A twice-a-week tour to the Stockyards leaves from the Radisson Plaza Hotel opposite the Convention Center at 2:45 P.M. every Tuesday and Saturday. Other trips departing from Dallas points go to Dallas landmarks, South Fork Ranch, Grapevine, and other popular regional sites.

710 East Davis	972-263-0274
Grand Prairie, Texas 75050	214-630-1000
www.coachusa.com	

City Bus: "THE T"

Getting around in Fort Worth requires wheels. If you don't own any, The T, Fort Worth's excellent bus system, can get you almost anywhere you want to go. If there is no regular route to your destination, call 817-215-8600 for "Rider Request" service.

Customer Service Center	817-215-8600
800 Houston Street	
Fort Worth, Texas 76102	

Horse-drawn Carriages

How about a moonlight ride in an open-air, horse-drawn carriage through the streets of the city? Classic Carriages is the way to go. Departing from the Worthington Hotel (200 Main Street), these pleasant fifteen-minute rides take you through the Sundance Square area. They operate on a first-come, first-served basis, weather and street closure permitting, from 7:30 P.M. to midnight. The cost is $20 for one to four passengers and $5 for each additional rider.

With a bit of advance planning, the carriages can be reserved for a special occasion. These thirty-minute trips pick up and drop you off anywhere in the downtown Fort

Worth area. The cost is $95 and they are available seven days a week, 24 hours a day.

Stable at Sundance   817-336-0400
www.classic-carriages.com   E-mail: buckfarm@flash.net

Tarantula

Traveling back and forth from Grapevine to the Stockyard Station in Fort Worth's northside, this restored steam train evokes memories of the Old West. Those were the days when the people of Fort Worth tried to attract commercial transportation to the city. When the first few rail lines were shown on an old map someone noticed a similarity between a tarantula and the shape of the radiating track routes. Somehow the name stuck. Now, we have a Tarantula Train touring the northeast section of Tarrant County.

Photo courtesy of J. Reagan Ferguson

The Cooke Locomotive Works of Patterson, New Jersey, built engine 2248 ("Puffy") in 1896. It was used as a fire control "pumper" in Northern California and later as a ceremonial engine for the Southern Pacific Railroad. When it was retired, a private collector purchased it. Later sold to the Texas State Railroad and used briefly in the 1970s, 2248 was acquired in 1990 by Tarantula and restored at a cost of $1 million. It is the *only* operational steam locomotive in Texas dating from before the turn of the *last* century and appears likely to be functional into the *next* century.

Puffy pulls four 1925 day coaches finished in 1908 décor and two 1927 touring coaches with similar styling. The touring coaches have arches with wrought iron railings along their sides rather than windows. During the winter months (days?) windows are installed for passenger comfort.

Stockyards Station	**Cotton Belt Depot**
140 E. Exchange Avenue, A-350	707 South Main Street
Fort Worth, Texas 76106	Grapevine, Texas 76051
817-625-7245	FAX: 817-740-1119
www.tarantulatrain.com	

Schedule:

Wednesday-Saturday	Depart Grapevine 10:00 A.M.
	Arrive Stockyards 11:15 A.M.
	Depart Stockyards 2:00 P.M.
	Arrive Grapevine 3:15 P.M.
Friday-Saturday	Depart Grapevine 6:00 P.M.
	Arrive Stockyards 7:15 P.M.
	Depart Stockyards 10:15 P.M.
	Arrive Grapevine 11:30 P.M.
Sunday	Depart Grapevine 1:00 P.M.
	Arrive Stockyards 2:15 P.M.
	Depart Stockyards 4:45 P.M.
	Arrive Grapevine 6:00 P.M.

Fares:
Grapevine to Stockyards
Adult $22 round trip/ $13 one way, Senior (65+) $20 round trip/ $13 one way, Child (2-12) $11 round trip/ $10 one way

Groups discounted. Field trips further discounted. (Minimum of 20 children and one adult for every ten children.)

Soaring Adventures of America

Here's a really exciting way to see Fort Worth and the surrounding area. Gliders and hot air balloons give you a bird's eye view. Soaring Adventures is based in Connecticut but has facilities all over the country. The gliders take off from airports in McKinney and Caddo Mills. A two-year-old child can go up with a parent and an eight-year-old is permitted to go alone (*with* a pilot, of course).

Hot air balloons launch from Plano for one-hour flights. There are no age restrictions, but the passengers must be able to stand for the entire time (no babes in arms) and, of course, they should be tall enough to see out of the basket. Purchase gift certificates through the toll-free number and redeem them at take-off. Watch the newspaper for discount specials. *Fly high!*

1-800-SOARING (762-7464)   www.800soaring.com

Chapter 13

Shopping

Many a weekend is reserved for America's national pastime—SHOPPING. Texas has elevated this "sport" to a fine art with the country's most remarkable malls. Some are so spectacular they have become the destination, with the shops only secondary.

The inclusion of upscale restaurants and "food courts" can turn a trip to the store into a full day's outing. Brands from around the world have established outlets where discounted or "second" quality merchandise is available. Only in Texas could such emporia assemble into "Outlet Malls." Naturally, this has been copied all over the country.

Malls

Mall: What was originally a tree-lined promenade in St. James Park in London has evolved through time and space into an enclosed walkway lined with stores and filled with people.

The shopping mall is a Texas invention. Even if the first one was not built in the Lone Star State (and many people believe Northpark Mall in Dallas *was* the first—it opened in 1965), Texans have reinvented shopping with places like the Gallerias (Houston and Dallas) and the Parks in Arlington.

Grapevine Mills Mall

With the 1998 opening of the world's largest outlet mall, the reinvention continued. Featuring a mix of outlet stores, primary retail, and restaurants, this "miracle mile" can excite and occupy the entire family for days at a time.

Grapevine Mills is organized into six "neighborhoods," which are number-coded to the parking lots and keyed to a significant entry sculpture (football, wine barrel, twister, bluebonnet, *etc.*). If you can remember the image, you should be able to find your car and avoid having to spend too many days "in the neighborhood."

The main entry, denoted by the flags of the United States and Texas, brings the visitor in past the Rainforest Café. Here, the kids will be entertained by talking parrots and nature guides, teaching about the animals of the tropical rain forest, while waiting in line. Adjacent to the café is a gift shop selling jungle mementos—clothes, toys, and snacks— to keep the experience alive.

Dozens of shops sell toys, books, gifts, and clothing for children, while others have plenty for the grown-ups to peruse.

Bass Pro Shops

It is not unreasonable for the largest mall to be associated with the world's largest sporting goods store. Where else could a fisherman try out a fly rod in an actual trout stream without leaving the shop? Fly-tying demonstrations and lessons are available, too.

Like golf? Try before you buy on the putting green and driving range right at the store.

Camping enthusiast? You'll find every item you can think of in the Outdoor World camping section. Canoeing, kayaking, and climbing gear is here, as well.

Need a boat or RV? They have a huge collection of new and used vehicles of all varieties. Plan to stay awhile when you come. It will be difficult to pull the kids away.

2501 Bass Pro Drive   972-724-2018
Grapevine, Texas 76051   www.basspro.com
Hours: Monday-Saturday 9 A.M.-10 P.M., Sunday 10 A.M.-7 P.M.
Closed Christmas Day

Hulen Mall

Anchored by Dillard's, Foley's, and Montgomery Ward, the recently enlarged Hulen Mall has hundreds of stores selling shoes, sporting goods, shoes, jewelry, electronics, shoes, apparel, home furnishings, shoes, books, toys, shoes, gifts, luggage, and shoes.

An airy food court set beneath a lofty skylight provides a relaxing spot to take a break from breaking the bank. The renovations that added the wing containing Dillard's also brought a large number of covered parking spaces to shelter your vehicle from the broiling Texas summer sun.

The Premier Shopper Club (membership is free) makes shopping more convenient and valuable with special offers, discounts, and services such as free use of strollers, shopping bags, gift wrap, local phone calls at the Customer Service Center, and "members-only" special events.

How to get there: Exit 433 from I-20. Go south on Hulen Street. The main entrance is on the right just past Colter's Barbecue.

4800 South Hulen Street   817-294-1200
Fort Worth, Texas 76132   www.hulenmall.com
Hours: Monday-Saturday 10 A.M.-9 P.M., Sunday noon-6 P.M.

Ridgmar Mall

In the midst of a $70 million renovation as this goes to press, Ridgmar is evolving into what its management calls an "Un-mall." The final outcome must wait until 2001, but the plan is a series of territories to be called "Districts," each centered about one or more major retailers.

The **Arts and Fashion District** plans balconies over a wide plaza and a grand boulevard lined with quality boutiques between Foley's and Tarrant County's only Neiman Marcus.

The **Sports District** will feature a soft rubber floor with a court design and an electric scoreboard top center to display scores of athletic contests. Sporting goods and athletic apparel will be prominent features in this district's shops.

The **Kids District** centers on a fountain area with turtle sculptures. The ceiling will have a sky mural, and a biplane dangles from it. An ice cream cart serving sweet snacks should keep everyone happy—except Mom who will have to clean up the drips.

Ridgmar's walking club, the Sneaker Society, holds special events featuring speakers from All Saints Sportscare— Customer Service has a calendar—and membership benefits such as mall discounts, T-shirts, and reduced-cost health screening. Kids can walk with the grown-ups.

As the renovation progresses, AMC will add eighteen screens at Ridgmar Mall to the moviegoers' options in Fort Worth (See Chapter 15).

How to get there: West on I-30 from downtown Fort Worth. Exit at Green Oaks Road or Highway 183. North to Mall entrances.

2060 Green Oaks Road
I-30 and Green Oaks Road
Fort Worth, Texas 76116

817-731-0856
www.ridgmar.com

The Parks at Arlington

Dillard's, Foley's, and J.C. Penney are the big dogs at The Parks, but the little shoppers will enjoy Young at Heart Children's Shop, Radio Shack, Amy's Hallmark, and Love from Texas. B Dalton Bookseller has lots of kidstuff. Carlton Cards carries greetings for friends and family. With 153 store to choose among, no one will be bored except baby.

Food interludes include Wendy's Old Fashioned Hamburgers, Chick-Fil-A, and Frullati Café.

Located at I-20 and Highway 157.

3811 South Cooper Street
Arlington, Texas 76015
Hours extended during Christmas Season

817-467-2757
www.generalgrowth.com

North East Mall

At more than one hundred shops and food purveyors you'll find toys, clothing, books, jewelry, and, of course, shoes. Dillard's, Sears, J.C. Penney, and Wards are the anchor stores. But Saks Fifth Avenue and Nordstrom will open in the fall of 2000. Try Wherehouse Music, Waldenkids, or World of Science to find interesting kid-oriented products. The Children's Place has clothes and gifts for all ages. Or visit The Disney Store; surely, you know what you'll find there.

With MallPerks, an annual membership fee of $5 entitles you to earn points, which can be redeemed for items in their Rewards Portfolio. Purchases earn one point for every dollar spent at *any* of the 145 Simon Properties Malls nationwide and there are three others in this area. You can join online at the Simon website (www.simon.com).

How to get there: Located at Highway 121/183 and Loop 820 North. Exit from 121/183 at Bedford-Euless Road going south. At Melbourne Road turn left. From North Richland Hills or north Fort Worth take Loop 820 eastbound and exit at Pipeline Road. The mall will be on the right.

1101 Melbourne Road   817-284-3427
Hurst, Texas 76053   www.simon.com
Hours: Monday-Saturday 10 A.M.-9 P.M., Sunday noon-6 P.M.
Extended during the Christmas Holiday Season, Thanksgiving through January 1.

Festival Marketplace Mall

Formerly Forum 303 Mall, built more than twenty years ago, it has inaugurated a new idea in shopping. Instead of stores, the entire place is a series of booths selling discounted and antique merchandise. Come to roam and see if you can find a treasure.

2900 East Pioneer Parkway @ SH 360   817-213-1000
Arlington, Texas 76010   No website yet

Six Flags Mall

Start with Dillard's, Foley's, or Sears.

For the kids: Kay Bee Toy, Model Trains Arlington, T-shirts Plus.

Cards and gifts: Beary Patch, May's Hallmark, Carlton Cards, Spencer Gifts, Waldenbooks.

Music: Sam Goody, Wherehouse Music.

Movies: Tinseltown USA 9 (you guessed it: nine screens).

Plus: Adventure Dome Toy Ride.

Six Flags Mall Playtime and Step Two Children's Play Area are situated between the entrances to Sears and Foley's.

Mall Walkers Club: inquire at Customer Service.

2911 East Division   817-640-1641
Arlington, Texas 76011
Hours: Monday-Saturday 10 A.M.-9 P.M., Sunday noon-6 P.M.

North Hills Mall

Major department stores include Mervyn's California and
Stripling and Cox. The kids will be entertained for hours in
the Triple Play Gameroom (817-284-9696). Kay Bee Toys
and Hobby will have something for everyone. And anyone
feeling blue can be cheered up with something sweet from
The Candy Barrel.

Amy's Hallmark, B Dalton, and Waldenbooks provide materials to write on and read.

7624 Grapevine Highway   817-589-2236
North Richland Hills, Texas 76180

University Park Village

Although not a mall in the strictest sense, this outdoor promenade is lined with shops of a pleasing diversity and features
Starbuck's for coffee, The Water Street SeaFood Company,
the Blue Mesa Grill, and Chili's for dining. Stores include
Harold's and Talbot's. Bulldog's Kidswear, Mimi Maternity,
and Toys Unique are great places to get stuff for new babies,
expectant parents, and toddlers. Cowboys and Angels offers
"unique crafts and more."

Gap Kids and Uncommon Angels have more good stuff for
those in the family way. Barnes and Nobles BookStore,
Williams Sonoma, and a grown-up Gap round out the south
side.

Don't forget the Omaha Steak Store! It's *the* place to buy
prime Nebraska beef.

Right across University the Good Eats Grill, Ol' South Pan-
cake House, and Romano's Macaroni Grill have ample
additional dining space. Wander a bit further south on

University to Owens Family Restaurant or Hoffbrau Steak House.

1612 South University Drive   817-654-0521

Tandy Center

Yes, there are shoe stores as well as luggage and clothing shops. But, they also have Bugle Boy and a Carter's for Kids, so you can clothe the tots, too. In addition, you'll find Toy Zone, Rocky Mountain Chocolate Factory, Sweet Express (ice cream and candy), Pretzelmania, *and* The Fort Worth Store where everything Fort Worth and many things Texas can be found.

Right in the middle of it all, The Ice at Outlet Square allows skaters a place for cooling off and burning calories (see Chapter 7).

Fort Worth Outlet Square   817-415-3720
100 Throckmorton Street   1-800-414-2817
Fort Worth, Texas 76102   www.fwoutlet.com
Hours: Monday-Thursday 10 A.M.-7 P.M.
Friday-Saturday 10 A.M.-9 P.M., Sunday noon-6 P.M.

In Dallas

It is seldom necessary to trek east to Big D but, for two special shopping spots, the trip can be worthwhile. And, when in downtown Dallas, if the ice skating bug strikes, Plaza of the Americas has a pleasant, rarely crowded rink surrounded by two levels of specialty shops and restaurants. Negotiating the guidelive.com website is relatively easy, even for a novice. Use the search box, spell out what you want to find, and click "Go."

Dallas NorthPark Center

At Central Expressway and Northwest Highway (Loop 12) is one of the best malls in Texas. Until the new Nordstrom opens in 2001, Neiman Marcus will reign in the top spot as the major department store at NorthPark. Dillard's, Foley's and J. C. Penney are the other anchors.

NorthPark, however, is for families. There are stores for everyone. Especially for youngsters you'll find Gap Kids and babyGap, Gymboree, Limited Too, Texas Kids, and Oilily. Then visit FAO Schwarz for any toy any kid ever dreamed of having. Follow up with a Little Taste of Texas to find many things with a Texas flavor. And, finally, take them to Le Theatre de Marionette. Who doesn't like puppets?

At various times of the year there are special presentations, peaking between Thanksgiving and Christmas with the NorthPark Christmas Parade, Santa, Camp Gingerbread, the SPCA holiday pavilion (pick out a pet!), and the Trains at NorthPark. They run from before Thanksgiving until after New Years Day near the entrance to FAO Schwarz. The nominal admission charge ($4 for adults, $3 for children and seniors) goes to benefit the Ronald McDonald House of Dallas. The trains travel on 2,500 feet of track passing reproductions of Mount Rushmore, Cape Canaveral, the Golden Gate Bridge, Times Square, and, of course, the Dallas skyline.

1030 NorthPark Center   214-361-6345
Dallas, Texas 75225   www.guidelive.com
Hours: Monday-Saturday 10 A.M.-9 P.M., Sunday noon-6 P.M.

Dallas Galleria

With almost two million square feet and more than two hundred stores, Galleria has been the largest mixed-use complex in the Metroplex since its completion in 1982. Three office towers, a four-hundred-thirty-one-room Westin Hotel, a five-screen General Cinema, a private sports club, and the famous Galleria Ice Center complement four levels of retail shops. At Christmas, the rink holds the world's largest decorated indoor tree, reaching four stories up from ice level and surrounded by restaurants and balconies overlooking the skaters.

Macy's, Nordstrom, and Saks Fifth Avenue are the anchor stores. They are joined by babyGap, GapKids, Laura Ashley Mother and Child, and Gymboree as well as Talbot's Kids & Babies, and Limited Too.

Dozens of specialty, candy, card and gift shops fill miles of walkways on four levels. The new, spectacular NASCAR Silicon Motor Speedway—on the third level near Nordstrom—features two fourteen-seat stations where participants in a giant twenty-minute video game simulator feel the thrills of NASCAR racing. This is only the third of its kind to open in the USA. This is for "kids of *ALL* ages."

13350 North Dallas Parkway   972-458-2700
Dallas, Texas 75240   www.guidelive.com
Hours: Monday-Saturday 10 A.M.-9 P.M., Sunday noon-6 P.M.

Plaza of the Americas
Americas Ice Garden

A small, but elegant facility with marble stairways and fountains. Lots of fast food and a candy shop on the upper level that gets the latest Beanie Babies® every week.

Treebeards Restaurant on the rink level serves plentiful Cajun cookin' for lunch, Monday-Friday, 11 A.M.-2 P.M.

700 N. Pearl St.   214-720-8080
Dallas, Texas 75201   www.guidelive.com
Skating Hours:
Monday-Wednesday 11 A.M.-5:30 P.M. & 8 P.M.-10 P.M.
Thursday 11 A.M.-5 P.M., Friday 11 A.M.-8 P.M.
Saturday 1 P.M.-8 P.M., Sunday noon-5 P.M.
Fees: $5 + $2 skate rental
$4 for children 4 and under or for anyone before noon Monday-Friday
Parking in the Plaza of the Americas Garage is $10 for all day.

Downtown FW

Wandering downtown will lead you to any number of surprising shops in addition to those mentioned herein. Take a day to stroll and see what you can find. Around Christmastime, visit Bass Performance Hall to pick out ornaments recapitulating aspects of this architectural marvel. Right across the street is one of Fort Worth's Barnes and Nobles bookstores. A huge selection of children's books awaits the curious.

Downtown Dallas

There is only one reason to go to downtown Dallas if you are shopping:

Neiman Marcus Number ONE

The Flagship of the Neiman Marcus line, this one opened in 1907 by Herbert Marcus and A. L. and Carrie Marcus Neiman. More than ninety years later it is still a trendsetter in fashion merchandising. Numerous special events make it an exciting experience with something for shoppers of all ages.

One Marcus Square, 1618 Main Street   214-741-6911
Dallas, TX 75201   www.neimanmarcus.com

Nearby Outlets

A short drive away to the north or south and more outlet stores appear. Prime Retail Outlets operates the Gainesville and Hillsboro centers plus another south of Austin in San Marcos, Texas. Their website tells of special offers and events.

They also have centers in Plano (972-881-0019) and North Dallas (972-385-6183). Grapevine Mills is a Prime Outlets facility, too.

Southwest Outlet Center

More than ninety stores discounting name brands.

I-35 South, Exit 368   254-582-9205
Hillsboro, Texas 76645   FAX: 254-582-1911
www.primeoutlets.com
Hours vary from store to store.
Usually: Monday-Saturday 10 A.M.-8 P.M., Sunday 11 A.M.-6 P.M.

Gainesville Factory Shops

More than eighty shops.

I-35 North at Route 1202   940-668-1888
Gainesville, Texas 76240   Toll-free 1-888-545-7420
www.primeoutlets.com   FAX: 940-668-1988
Hours: Monday-Saturday 10 A.M.-6 P.M., Sunday 11 A.M.-6 P.M.
Weekday hours extended to 7 P.M. in January and February.

Denton Factory Stores/Exposition Mills

Located about an hour north of Fort Worth, slightly beyond Denton and including Carter's children's clothing, Levi's, Dockers, and Gadzooks outlets among many others. Bring a checkbook for bargains and an appetite. Good Eats Café is located right as you enter the shopping area.

I-35 at Loop 288   817-565-5040
Denton, Texas 76201
Hours: Monday-Saturday 9 A.M.-9 P.M., Sunday 11 A.M.-6 P.M.

Clothing

Kids 'R' Us

Like Toys 'R' Us, found all over the place. Lots of clothes and accessories for the crib-to-bicycle set. Find them in the Yellow Pages.

Old Navy

Home of the Performance Fleece. Every kid knows what that is. Parents do, too. Old Navy sells for all ages and tastes. The website locates stores and has games for the kids—the adults will not be able to keep up—and coloring pages for the printer. There's also information about the characters in the TV Ads.

5000 South Hulen Street   817-263-7500
Fort Worth, Texas 76132   www.oldnavy.com
1-800-OLD-NAVY (1-800-653-6289)

Five other stores in the area. Check website or Yellow Pages under "Clothing."

Kid to Kid

Started in Sandy, Utah, this has become a national franchise with stores in thirteen states. Their specialty is recycling "gently used" toys and children's clothing.

The pink child-size door adjacent to the grown-up entry shows their focus on kids. You may be surprised at what they carry—excellent cribs turn up regularly—as the stock is always changing.

4750 Bryant Irvin Road   817-263-4660
Fort Worth, Texas 76132   www.kidtokid.com

Cowboy Boots/Western Wear

Boot Town

Boots for grown-ups; boots for kids. Justin, Nocona, Tony Lama, Wrangler. Your choice. And hats and jeans and belts to go with 'em.

2901 Alta Mere (at I-30)   4115 South Cooper (at I-20)
Fort Worth, Texas   Arlington, Texas
817-654-2668   817-784-8082

1105 West Pipeline Road (at Melbourne)
Hurst, Texas
817-589-0109
Hours: Monday-Saturday 9 A.M.-9 P.M., Sunday noon-6 P.M.

Cavender's Boot City

Everything for the lil' buckaroos and buckarettes. And for grown-up cowboys (or wannabes), too.

5248 South Hulen Street	857 West Pipeline Road
Fort Worth, Texas 76132	Hurst, Texas 76053
817-294-4400	817-595-0462
	Metro 817-589-2180
3308 East Pioneer Parkway	2515 Centennial Drive
Arlington, Texas 76010	Arlington, Texas 76011
817-633-2324	817-640-8899
Metro 817-6408838	
www.cavenders-boot-city.com	

Sheplers

The world's largest western stores and catalog. Call the toll-free number for a catalog or pick one up in either of the Metroplex stores. There are stores in Austin, Amarillo, San Antonio, and Oklahoma City, as well.

Arlington	**Mesquite**
2500 East Centennial Drive	18500 LBJ Freeway
817-640-5055	972-270-8811
www.sheplers.com	1-800-242-6540

Toys & Dolls

While an entire volume could be devoted to the toy stores in the Metroplex, a few deserve mention here.

Toy Works

There once was a store called Chadd's Rainbow. It started with a dream and grew too fast. When Chadd's Rainbow folded, its Fort Worth store, under the guidance of Winnie

Elmore, became Toy Works. Now operated by Winnie's daughter and son-in-law, Nancy and Art Hay, Toy Works continues to sell educational toys and games to challenge and promote the developing child's physical and mental skills.

6100 Camp Bowie   817-737-8697
Fort Worth, Texas 76116

Toys 'R' Us

The monster chain toy store with all the latest at the best prices. Lots of locations. Check the Yellow Pages.

Kay Bee

Found in just about every mall in the area. Also carries hobby stuff.

Bookstores

All kinds and all over, but some are more famous than others. Some also offer special amenities. Bookstop has coffeepots (flavored and regular) for free fill-ups while browsing. The children's section has a cozy reading area.

Borders solves the hunger and thirst problem with an in-store coffee bar that serves drinks and deserts. This is also the spot for regular, open microphone poetry readings. Several reader/writer groups hold meetings at Borders "periodically." Check out Cowtown Crimesolvers, Freelance Writers, and Sisters in Crime.

Barnes and Noble sponsors Storytime for children (see Chapter 8) in many of its numerous local stores. There are a dozen Barnes and Noble bookstores in the Metroplex.

Bookstop

A top discount chain selling everything at least 10 percent below list price. With the *Readers Choice* membership card (for a small annual fee) an additional 10 percent discount is given, making New York Times best sellers 40 percent off. Barnes and Noble has been the parent company since 1988, so find Bookstop on the web at BN.COM.

There are stores in most major cities, recognizable by the red and white octagon sign. The children's section is large, well stocked, and offers seating for quiet reading.

4801 South Hulen Street
Fort Worth, Texas 76132
817-346-9055
www.bn.com

Bookstop/Inwood Village
5550 W. Lovers Lane, #147
Dallas, Texas 75209
214-357-2697

Bookstop/Mesquite
1765 N. Towne East Boulevard, Suite 109
Mesquite, Texas 75150
Hours: Monday-Saturday 10 A.M.-10 P.M.

Barnes and Noble

In addition to these, there are Barnes and Noble bookstores in Grapevine, Lewisville, Irving, Dallas, Plano, Richardson, and Mesquite.

Downtown
401 Commerce Street
Fort Worth, Texas 76102
817-332-7178
Hours: Monday-Thursday 10 A.M.-9 P.M.
Friday-Saturday 10 A.M.-midnight, Sunday 11 A.M.-8 P.M.

www.BN.com

University Village
1612 South University Drive, #401
Fort Worth, Texas 76107
817-335-2791

South Arlington
3909 South Cooper Street
Arlington, Texas 76015
817-557-1171

North Richland Hills
8525 Airport Freeway
North Richland Hills, Texas 76180
817-281-7042

North Arlington
934 East Copeland Road
Arlington, Texas 76011-4944
817-277-5184

Hours: Monday-Saturday 9 A.M.-11 P.M., Sunday 10 A.M.-10 P.M.

Borders Books & Music

With stores strategically placed around the area, Borders provides places to browse, read, watch movies, drink coffee, and chat with friends before heading home with your favorite reading matter.

Books, music, periodicals, videos, and good coffee all under one roof. In addition to the Metroplex stores listed, there are two stores each in Austin and San Antonio and many more scattered across the United States.

Find them on the Internet at www.borders.com.

Fort Worth   817-390-9473
Across from Hulen Mall
4613 South Hulen Street
Fort Worth, Texas 76132
Hours: Monday-Saturday 9 A.M.-11 P.M., Sunday 9 A.M.-9 P.M.

Lewisville   972-459-2321
At the corner of I-35 and Round Grove Road
Adjacent to Vista Ridge Mall
2403 South Stemmons, Suite 100
Lewisville, Texas 75067
Hours: Monday-Saturday 9 A.M.-11 P.M., Sunday 9 A.M.-9 P.M.

Dallas   214-739-1166
In Old Town Shopping Center at Lovers Lane and Greenville Avenue
5500 Greenville Avenue
Dallas, Texas 75206
Hours: Monday-Saturday 9 A.M.-11 P.M., Sunday 9 A.M.-9 P.M.

In Preston Oaks Shopping Center   214-363-1977
At the Southeast corner of Preston Road and Royal Lane
10720 Preston Road, Suite 1018
Dallas, Texas 75230
Hours: Monday-Saturday 9 A.M.-11 P.M., Sunday 10 A.M.-9 P.M.

Plano   972-713-9857
At the Southwest corner of Preston and Park
1601 Preston Road, Suite J
Plano, Texas 75093
Hours: Monday-Saturday 9 A.M.-11 P.M., Sunday 9 A.M.-9 P.M.

Half-Price Books

Started in a Dallas laundromat in 1974, Half Price Books has burgeoned and now has stores in eight states, all of which buy used books, videos, records (remember them?), CDs, cassettes, and other printed material with the exception of "yesterday's newspaper." Now stocking a selection of new gift items, they make Christmas shopping easy. Gift certificates from any Half Price Books can be used at any Half Price Books.

With a constantly changing inventory, each location offers a new adventure for the seeker after knowledge or reading relaxation.

There are fourteen Half Price Books in the Metroplex. The newest is a 7,000 square-foot store in Lewisville (Vista Ridge Mall). Look for the Children's section—Half Pint Books—in each store.

Half Price Books has a summer reading program for children 15 and under. The *Half Pint Library* program has collected books all over the country to help stock libraries in hospitals and community centers.

5264 South Hulen Street   817-294-1166
Fort Worth, Texas 76132
Hours: Monday-Thursday 9:30 A.M.-10 P.M.
Friday-Saturday 9:30 A.M.-11 P.M., Sunday 10 A.M.-8 P.M.

6912 Ridgmar Meadow Road   817-732-4111
Fort Worth, Texas
www.halfpricebooks.com
Hours: Monday-Saturday 9 A.M.-10 P.M., Sunday 11 A.M.-8 P.M.
Holiday hours may vary. Call to verify.
Two in Arlington, one in Bedford, and one in Irving.

The Book Rack

Another pair of places to recycle used books. The Book Rack accepts trades and will give you one book for each pair you bring at the same cover price. Most paperback books sell for about half the original price. They also carry comics, hardback, and audio books.

2304 W Park Row	5210 Rufe Snow Drive
Arlington, Texas 76013	North Richland Hills, Texas 76180
817-274-1717	817-656-5565

B. Dalton

Multiple sites—look in every mall.

Waldenbooks

Ditto.

The Black Bookworm

Sonia Williams-Babers owns this shop featuring books by African-American authors, books about Black history, Black life, Black social issues. For readers of *all* colors.

605 East Berry Street, Suite 110   817-923-9661
On the I-35 access road at the NW corner of Berry.
Fort Worth, Texas 76110
E-mail: blackbookworm@yahoo.com
Hours: Monday-Thursday 11 A.M.-7 P.M., Friday-Saturday 11 A.M.-6 P.M.

Christian Book Stores

Logos

This charming, one-of-a-kind bookstore sells books and gifts, most with a religious flavor. It carries an excellent selection of children's books with secular as well as biblical themes.

3105 A Winthrop Street   817-732-5070
Fort Worth, Texas 76116   1-800-30-LOGOS (305-6467)
www.LOGOSBOOKSTORE.NET   E-mail: logosfw@airmail.net
Hours: Monday-Friday 10 A.M.-6 P.M., Saturday 10 A.M.-5 P.M.

Cokesbury's

A little store almost hidden a few blocks from the TCU campus. Look on the north side of Berry.

2720 W. Berry Street   817-926-5313
Fort Worth, Texas 76109

Crafts

When the rains come, and they always do, there are often hours that must be filled to maintain sanity. Plan ahead and have some activities delineated to keep little fingers busy. Here are some of the best places to find the projects.

Hobby Town USA

Everything for the hobbyist from model building supplies to toy trains in all sizes. A second store is at 3701 S. Cooper, Arlington, 76015, 817-557-2225.

5276 South Hulen Street   817-263-1196
Fort Worth, Texas 76132

Hobby Lobby

Thirteen stores in the Metroplex assure everyone of access to modeling, leather, candles, painting, art and woodworking supplies, pottery, and dried or artificial flowers. And baskets, baskets, baskets. Holiday hours are usually abbreviated so call to be sure.

The website has printable discount coupons.

4628-A South Cooper Street   817-557-8446
Arlington, Texas 76017   www.hobbylobby.com
Hours: Monday-Saturday 9 A.M.-8 P.M., Sunday noon-6 P.M.

620 South West Wilshire Boulevard   817-295-5476
Burleson, Texas 76028
Hours: Monday-Friday 9 A.M.-8 P.M., Saturday 9 A.M.-6 P.M.
Sunday noon-6 P.M.

More in Carrollton, Denton, Lewisville, Irving, Southlake, Dallas, Mesquite, Plano, Allen, Sherman, Cedar Hill, and Rockwall and in 23 other states.

Michael's MJDesigns

After a near-disastrous over-expansion, Michael's MJDesigns has retrenched and is under new management in eight Metroplex locations. Go to the website to see the current sales offerings.

Ridgmar
1400 Green Oaks Road
Ft. Worth, Texas 76116
(817) 737-3668
www.mjdesigns.com
Hours: Monday-Saturday 9 A.M.-9 P.M., Sunday 11 A.M.-6 P.M.

Grapevine
1250 William D Tate
Grapevine, Texas 76051
(817) 251-0099

Similar merchandise to that found in Hobby Lobby is available in these large, bright stores. Other FW/D sites include:

MJDesigns Lewisville   972-315-9046
2325 S. Stemmons Suite #106
MJDesigns Preston   214-696-5491
810 Preston Forest Shopping Ctr
MJDesigns Carrollton   972-662-3402
3407 Trinity Mills Road
MJDesigns Mockingbird   214-827-2965
6120 E. Mockingbird Lane
MJDesigns Plano East   972-578-9600
600 W. 15th Street
MJDesigns Duncanville   972-780-8913
335 South Cedar Ridge

Cooper Street Craft Mall

Hundreds of artisans under on roof. Also, find retail gifts including Russ stuffed animals and Ty Beanie Babies®, not to mention wonderful scented candles and more.

1701 South Cooper Street   817-261-3184
Arlington, Texas 76010

Hours: Monday-Wednesday 10 A.M.-6 P.M.
Thursday-Saturday 10 A.M.-8 P.M., Sunday noon-5 P.M.

Leathercraft

In cattle country, someone's always needing or making something out of leather. Here's how to find the supplies.

Tandy Leather

This division of the Radio Shack empire has closed its retail stores, much to the sorrow of many loyal customers. However, Tandy still sells leather and related materials through its catalog by mail or over the Internet. Call 1-888-890-1611 to request a catalog or to place orders. Ordering online is easy, too. Visit the web site at www.TandyLeather.com.

The Leather Factory

A huge warehouse with everything for the leather crafter from hides, dyes, and tools to precut pieces, kits, stamping supplies, and decorative hardware (buckle sets, conchos, and beads). For big spenders, they offer a club membership, which allows purchases at wholesale prices for a small annual fee ($25). The Leather Factory also markets to professionals and resellers, so expect to find almost anything you might need. Their catalog is extensive. Schools and hospitals also get wholesale pricing.

How to get there: From Loop 820 take the Eastland Road exit and get on the northbound access road. The Leather Factory is just south of Berry Street on the eastside of 820.

3847 East Loop 820 South	817-496-4874
P.O. Box 50429	1-800-433-3201
Fort Worth, Texas 76105	FAX: 817-496-9806

Hide Crafter Leathercraft

This new company (entering its fourth year), which sells locally and ships worldwide to hobbyists of all skill levels, is owned and operated by experienced leather crafters. There are educational programs offered at the store (call for details), and it is also host to the Lone Star Leathercrafters Guild. Ask Andy Stasiak for details. He's president of the guild and general manager of the company.

2017B White Settlement Road   817-878-5797
Fort Worth, Texas 76107   FAX: 817-878-5795
www.hidecrafter.com   E-mail: hcrafter@flash.net

Bicycles

All major chain (Wal-Mart, K-Mart, Target, Service Merchandise) and department stores sell bikes. Here are a few other places to purchase and get them properly maintained and assembled:

Bikes USA

A complete sales and service bicycle shop located next to Service Merchandise across from Hulen Mall. Also has locations in Arlington (900 E. Copeland Rd., 76011, Cooper and I-30, 817-861-0388) and North Richland Hills (7517 Grapevine Highway, 76180, across from North Hills Mall, 817-281-1211).

5000 South Hulen Street   817-346-2266
Fort Worth, Texas 76132

Bicycles, Inc

Another source for all things bicyclic. Sales, repair, and financing available in the stores. Two other area sites: Southwest Fort Worth (5039 Granbury Road, 76133, 817-292-2911) and Arlington (1607 S. Bowen, 76013, 817-461-5555). They guarantee to match all locally advertised prices and give lifetime free service.

510-1 Harwood   817-268-6572
Bedford, Texas 76021   www.bicyclesinc.com

Sporting Goods

Too many to name. Every mall has at least one selling athletic shoes, clothing, uniforms, and accessories. The store for everything is:

Oshman's

The are fourteen stores around the Metroplex, including Denton and Tyler.

Outdone only by Bass Pro's Outdoor World, this chain of sporting goods superstores has everything for the athlete and sports enthusiast.

Fort Worth stores near Hulen Mall at Overton Park Plaza (817-377-1515) and Ridgmar Town Square (817-731-8578) are joined by one near Irving Mall (972-986-1110) and another in Denton at Golden Triangle Mall (940-566-3902).

Another great chain is **ACADEMY**, with scattered locations. Check the yellow pages and the Sunday papers.

Hallmark

Once upon a time it was all about greeting cards. Now, however, Hallmark is party trimmings, tree ornaments, Beanie Babies®, and Star Wars!

There is a Gold Crown Store in almost every mall and many in other shopping centers, but the friendliest people and the best service is at:

Norman's Hallmark 817-294-8808
4620 Bryant Irvin Road
Cityview Shopping Centre
Fort Worth, Texas 76132

Candy

Got a craving for chocolate? Look no further.

Sweet Shop USA
Mrs. Prindible
American Caramel

The factory is in the back. Out front, find all the confectionery combinations any chocoholic could covet. Truffles in every variety share counter space with the best almond bark anywhere! Look for the specials on the tables with grab bags and broken pieces. Buy it by the pound.

625 Stayton Street   817-332-7941
Fort Worth, Texas 76107
Hours: Monday-Friday 9 A.M.-6 P.M., Saturday 10 A.M.-4:30 P.M.

Nuts

Texas is pecan country. Get 'em at Vending Nut Company (see Chapter 10). Or call Durham-Ellis Pecan Company (1-800-732-2629).

People Gotta Eat

Perhaps the best way to say "Nuts to you" to your friends and family. The Killer Pecans are exactly that. Keep water handy to put out the fire. Telephone orders are taken Monday-Friday, 9 A.M.-5 P.M. Central Time. Visa, MasterCard, Discover, and American Express accepted.

P.O. Box 191229   214-747-3500
Dallas, Texas 75219   800-696-1131
www.peoplegottaeat.com   FAX: 214-747-0200

Leonard Farms

The place to go for farm-fresh Texas pecans. The orchard in Granbury is one of the largest in the world. It is smack in the middle of Pecan Plantation, a residential community, and a drive through the area gives a good view of the trees. Leonard Farms visits by agriculture students (usually college-level) may be prearranged with the management. Don't try to do it around the holidays in December, because everyone is at the stores selling, like, NUTS!

9500 Orchard Drive   817-579-6887
Granbury, Texas 76049   1-800-252-6887
FAX: 817-279-7057
Hours: Monday-Sunday 9 A.M.-6 P.M.

Fort Worth Store: 817-336-2566
2901 Cullen Street   Fax: 817-336-2563
Fort Worth, Texas 76107
Hours: Monday-Friday 10 A.M.-5 P.M.

Fireworks

Fireworks sales stands seem to spring up like mushrooms after rain every year in late May or June. They are situated in out-of-the-way spots along country roads where anyone can find them.

It is illegal to set off fireworks inside the city limits without a permit, so enjoy the professional displays all around the Metroplex. In Parker County, things are a bit more relaxed, but fire safety should be of paramount importance. In hot, dry summers like those of the past few years, grass fires start too easily when bottle rockets go astray.

Christmas

The Christmas Season used to begin—traditionally—on the Friday after Thanksgiving. These days stores begin to gear up for Santa and the Elves right after—sometimes *before*—Halloween. The Christmas Season now coincides with College Football. That makes sense since, in Texas, Santa wears Cowboy boots and hitches longhorns to the sleigh!

'tis the Season

The Christmas store. The place to go for decorations, lights, and artificial trees.

They'll permanently prewire the trees with lights for an additional fee. That leaves the decorating to you. There are four locations in the area. The mall stores open starting in late September, but the one at the Benbrook circle is open year round. As the countdown to Christmas begins (after Thanksgiving) hours are extended. And be prepared for a mouthwatering experience upon entering the main store. That's where they make the *FUDGE*!

Fort Worth   817-244-6420
3708 Benbrook Circle (Highway 377 S)
Hours: Monday-Thursday 10 A.M.-7 P.M.
Friday-Saturday 10 A.M.-9 P.M., Sunday noon-6 P.M.

Hulen Mall   **Arlington**
4800 South Hulen Street   Six Flags Mall
817-361-5780   817-274-0508

North Hills Mall
NE Loop 820 @ Grapevine Highway
817-284-3966
Hours: Monday-Saturday 10 A.M.-9 P.M., Sunday noon-6 P.M.

Another source for trees and trimming supplies with Dallas and Arlington showrooms:

Decorator's Warehouse

1535 South Bowen Road   2525 Royal Lane
Arlington, Texas   Dallas, Texas
817-460-4488   972-247-2959

Chapter 14

Cultural Activities

Opportunities to enjoy or participate in theater, dance, art, and music prevail all around the Metroplex. Fort Worth, Arlington, and the Mid-cities have numerous organizations displaying all forms of the performing arts.

Dallas has its own set of activities centered in the new arts district around the Morton H. Meyerson Concert Hall. More information is available in Kay McCasland Threadgill's book *Exploring Dallas with Children.*

Theater

Bass Performance Hall

This is the newest, most spectacular venue of its kind in Texas, perhaps the entire country. The superb acoustics and stunning décor make this theater a wonderful place to take in one of the many professional touring productions of original Broadway plays.

Since opening in 1998, Bass Hall has staged productions of *Phantom of the Opera, Miss Saigon,* and *Smokey Joe's Café,* among others. The *Big Apple Circus* ended the 1999 season.

The 2000 schedule includes *The Buddy Holly Story, Tap Dogs, Grease,* and *42nd Street.*

Ticket prices range from $24 to $64 for individual seats. Group discounts are available and season tickets are also at lower-than-single-performance price.

Performing Arts Fort Worth

The organization that manages Bass Performance Hall also presents an extensive and widely varied guest artist series. Presenting a diversified group of unique stage shows throughout the year, this organization will have something for every taste.

Bass Hall Theater

Dancers, drummers, acrobats, and musicians appear at Bass Hall Theater (see Chapter 16).

817-212-4280   1-888-597-STAR (7827)
www.basshall.com

Casa Manana

The "house of tomorrow" was the first permanent theater-in-the-round built in the USA. The original Casa Manana, Fort Worth's largest theater, built in 1936 by Billy Rose, had seriously deteriorated until 1957, when Mel Dacus promoted its rebirth as a geodesic dome.

Mr. Dacus served as general manager until 1975. He regularly appeared on the Casa stage as Tevye in *Fiddler on the Roof* and Baron Von Trapp in *The Sound of Music*. In recent years he was seen as Santa Claus in Casa's Christmas galas. He died October 6, 1999 at his home in Fort Worth. He was seventy-six.

The gleaming aluminum dome of Casa Manana is a Fort Worth landmark. In the forty years since its rebirth Casa has been the site of more than three hundred presentations of musical, comic, and dramatic theater, performances by singers, dancers, and comedians and, most significantly, children's theater.

Casa's Theater School trains the rising stars of the next generation in all aspects of theater production. Two three-week classes in June and July hold sessions two or three days a week for kids from 4-12. The cost per child is $189/class.

Casa Kids Outreach Program sends a troupe of students from the Theater School to entertain at nursing homes, hospitals, and area arts festivals for those unable to get to the theater.

With the opening of Bass Hall, many of the Casa Broadway productions will be seen at that new facility.

3101 Lancaster Avenue　　　　817-332-2272
Fort Worth, Texas 76107　　　www.casamanana.org
Box office hours: 9 A.M.-5 P.M.
Show Times: Friday 7:30 P.M., Saturday and Sunday 2 P.M.

William Edrington Scott Theater

The theater at the Modern Art Museum may be in flux while the MAM prepares to move to its new building. Call for information.

3505 West Lancaster Avenue　　　817-738-6509
Fort Worth, Texas 76107?

Hip Pocket Theater

This small theater company stages productions in an outdoor setting. Instead of air conditioning, they use fans and mist sprayers. In its twenty-third year of staging original and rarely performed works, Hip Pocket has done some remarkable things on a shoestring budget. They have staged over one hundred seventy-five plays, more than ninety of them world premieres.

Call or consult the website for information.

How to get there: Take North Loop 820 to Las Vegas Trail (west of Downtown Fort Worth) and go north on Las Vegas Trail. Turn right after you pass the church and that's Oak Acres.

1620 North Las Vegas Trail　　　817-246-9775

Fort Worth, Texas 76108   www.hippocket.org
Curtain: 9 P.M. June-August, 8:15 P.M. September-October

Shakespeare in the Park

A summer tradition in Trinity Park. Performances begin at 8:30 P.M. Enter at the Seventh Street side of the park. A merger between Stage West and Shakespeare in the Park, forming Allied Theater Group, took place October 1, 1999. The 2000 season will feature another offering of the Bard's work at Stage West (see below).

Fancy catered or plain box lunch meals can be arranged with reserved table seating or blankets on the grass.

For ticket information call 817-923-6698.

Fort Worth Theater

The Fort Worth Theater has been a part of life here since 1955. The Scott Theater at the Modern Art Museum was where its first productions (beginning around 1961) were seen. It relocated to Orchestra Hall in 1973.

4401 Trail Lake Drive   817-921-5300
Fort Worth, Texas 76109
www.star-telegram.com/home/fwt

Stage West

The theater is located across from Einstein's Bagels almost *on* the TCU campus. The 1999-2000 season is Stage West's twenty-first and the first as part of Allied Theater Group.

3055 South University Drive   817-784-9378
Fort Worth, TX 76109-5608   FAX: 817-926-8650
www.alliedtheater.org   E-mail: stgwest@ix.netcom.com
Box office hours: Tuesday-Saturday 9 A.M.-6 P.M.
Box office telephone answered evenings during performances and after 4 P.M. on Sundays.

Circle Theatre

An intimate auditorium seats only 125 audience members around an "open thrust" stage to view works by Texas and Southwest regional playwrights. In collaboration with local university theater departments, Circle gives students and college interns the opportunity to work in the environment of a professional theater. It was founded in 1981 and is now located in the basement of the old Sanger Building.

230 West Fourth Street   P.O. Box 470456
Fort Worth, Texas 76102   Fort Worth, Texas 76147-0456
817-877-3040   FAX: 817-877-3536
Office: 817-877-3848   www.circletheatre.com
Show Times: Thursday and Friday 7:30 P.M.
Saturday 4 P.M. and 8:30 P.M., "Sweetheart Sunday" 4 P.M.
Prices: Thursday evenings and all matinees $15
Friday and Saturday evenings $20

Jubilee Theatre

Another excellent small theater presenting high quality, sometimes provocative musical or dramatic works.

Call for additional information.

506 Main Street   817-338-4411
Fort Worth, Texas 76102
Show Times: Friday and Saturday evenings 8:15 P.M.
Sunday matinee 3:15 P.M.
Tickets: $10-$16

Theater Arlington

Technically a community theater, this production company is entering its twenty-seventh year of frequently professional caliber shows.

Call for information about performances, show times, outreach programs, and Theater Guild.

305 West Main   817-275-7661
Arlington, Texas 76010   Theater office 817/261-9628

www.theatrearlington.org
E-mail: theatrearlington@theatrearlington.org

Creative Arts Theatre & School

A training ground for the next generation of Cosettes, Annies, and Phantoms, CATS offers classes for ages four to adult in dance, theater (acting, directing, stage design), and other aspects of production. Summer classes are in two-week sessions.

Six productions are staged during the regular season (on the first two weekends of each month). The summer season runs for one week each in June, July, and August with performances at 10:30 in the morning.

Dallas has an extensive roster of theatrical opportunities both for viewing and participation. Kay McCasland Threadgill will start you off nicely in Chapter 3 of *Exploring Dallas with Children* (Republic of Texas Press, second edition, 1998).

1100 West Randol Mill Road	817-274-6047
Arlington, Texas 76012	Metro 817-265-8512
After hours 817-275-9956	817-861-CATS (2287)
Monday-Friday 10:30 A.M.-6 P.M.	

Teatro Main Street

The area's first Hispanic theater. Productions are staged with local and professional talent and are often in English one night and Spanish the next. Founded by Robin Medina Winnett, Teatro Main Street is housed in a Stockyards location that serves as office, rehearsal hall, and theater.

Call for schedule and performance dates.

1541 North Main Street   817-626-1969
Fort Worth, Texas

Music

Bass Performance Hall

Many of Fort Worth's divers musical and theatrical production companies have transferred their homes to this
spectacular structure. The angels on the façade trumpet
their joyous welcome to all attendees.

330 East Fourth Street   817-212-4200
Fourth and Calhoun Streets   Tickets: 817-212-4280
Fort Worth, Texas 76102   1-888-597-STAR (7827)
www.basshall.com

Fort Worth Symphony Orchestra
Fort Worth Symphony Pops Orchestra

The 1999-2000 season is Conductor John Giordano's last
with the Symphony. His final appearances was in May 2000,
with the Gala Farewell on May 20.

The Symphony season is divided into classical and pops
series.

330 East Fourth Street, Suite 200   817-665-6000
Fort Worth, Texas 76102   FAX: 817-665-6100
www.fwsymphony.org

Concerts in the Garden

Each summer the Symphony does a set of open-air concerts
in the Fort Worth Botanic Garden. Check the website or call
in early spring to get details. A fireworks extravaganza
accompanies the July 4th appearance!

Fort Worth Opera

Performances are at Bass Hall. They sell out quickly, so plan
ahead. Tickets may be purchased for all three productions,
the second and third ("miniseries"), or singly. The best seats
go to season ticket holders.

Groups of ten or more benefit from discounts, priority seating, and a special welcome.

Single tickets may be purchased six weeks prior to a production. However, most performances sell out with season tickets. Prices range from $20-$75 per person for Friday and Saturday evening performances, and $18-$68 per person for the Sunday matinee.

Opera Sweets, the children's program of the Fort Worth Opera takes fully staged and costumed short (one act) productions to schools, malls, parks, and service organizations. Middle and high school students may attend Wednesday night dress rehearsals and receive an opera study guide.

Van Cliburn Piano International Competitions

The eleventh international competition will be held May 25-June 11, 2001; the twelfth international competition will be held May 20-June 5, 2005; and the thirteenth international competition will be held May 22-June 7, 2009.

Sponsored by the Cliburn Foundation (www.cliburn.org), once every four years the world's greatest pianists compete for the biggest prize since Mr. Cliburn returned from the then Soviet Union in 1959 as winner of the Tchaikovsky Piano Competition.

Host families furnish housing for the international aggregation of stellar visitors who descend upon Fort Worth. The *Star-Telegram* devotes pages to biographies and timetables of events. The final days can be quite frenetic.

Van Cliburn Piano Competition for Talented Amateurs

This event premiered in 1999 and was such a resounding success that it will become a regular feature of the Cliburn circuit. The next cycle occurs June 5-10, 2000, after which it

will become biennial so as to avoid conflict with the *BIG*
Cliburn (see above).

Cliburn Concerts

The same foundation that presents the world's leading piano
competition every four years in Fort Worth also produces an
impressive series of concerts featuring guest artists at Bass
Performance Hall. For information call 817-335-9000.

Texas Wind Symphony

Ray C. Lichtenwalter is director of bands and conductor of
the wind ensemble at the University of Texas at Arlington.
He has led the Texas Wind Symphony, a professional wind
ensemble, since 1987. The subscription concert series at
Bass Performance Hall runs from September through May.

Incidentally, Dallas has a Wind Symphony, too. They perform at the Morton H. Meyerson Concert Center. Look them
up on the web at www.dws.org.

2225 East Randol Mill Road, Suite 407   817-633-2877
Arlington, Texas 76011   FAX: 817-788-2697
E-mail: txws@swbell.net

Choral Music

Schola Cantorum of Texas

Now in its thirty-seventh season, Schola Cantorum ends the
2000 season on May 21 at Bass Performance Hall. Because
this marks Schola director Gary Ebensberger's twenty-fifth
and final year, the final concert is entitled "They were very
good years."

Concerts take place at Irons Recital Hall in Arlington, Bass
Performance Hall in Fort Worth and in area churches
between October and May each year. The highlight is the
Christmas "Gift of Music" to the community, held the first
week of December at St. Stephen Presbyterian Church in

Fort Worth and Trinity United Methodist Church in Arlington.

Schola Cantorum of Texas is a 501(c) 3 Charitable Arts Organization. The sixty-voice choir ranges in age from twenty-two to sixty-five and presents musical selections alluring to children as well as to the more sophisticated patron.

Season ticket prices range from $37 for seniors and students to $200 for high rollers (platinum). Single tickets cost as little as $10 (up to $50).

Schola holds auditions each summer. Do you sing?

3505 W. Lancaster   817-737-5788
Fort Worth, Texas 76107   FAX: 817-731-0835
www.star-telegram.com/homes/schola/

Texas Boys' Choir

A world-famous organization that trains boys starting at age seven. The campus in Fort Worth provides a complete school program for grades four through twelve. Concert tours take them around the world. Call for information.

2925 Riverglen Drive   817-924-1482
Fort Worth, Texas 76109   Metro 817-429-0066

Texas Girls' Choir

Same for girls ages eight through sixteen.

4449 Camp Bowie Boulevard   817-732-8161
Fort Worth, Texas 76107

Dance

D/FW Ballet

Under the leadership of artistic director Benjamin Houk, the Fort Worth based company presents a season that includes *The Nutcracker* at Christmastime and a mixture of new and classic ballet jewels. The Fort Worth season runs through the fall at Bass Performance Hall. Fair Park Music Hall is the setting for the Dallas portion of the calendar beginning with *The Nutcracker* in December.

6845 Green Oaks Road	817-763-0207
Fort Worth, Texas 76116	FAX: 817-763-
Dallas Performances: 214-369-5024	www.fwdballet.com

Ballet Arlington

Performing at UTA (University of Texas at Arlington) Texas Hall, this local company, founded in 1997, mounted a noteworthy production of *The Nutcracker* with guest dancers from the Bolshoi Ballet in December 1999. For other productions, guest artists or international stars often join students and local professionals.

Russian ballerina Svetlana Stanova is the Artistic Director. Her husband, Nikolai Semikov, is Artistic Designer. Both danced with the Moscow Classical Ballet, and Nikolai was a principal dancer with the Bolshoi.

Tickets are available through Dillard's or by calling 1-800-654-9545.

1201 West Abram Street	817-459-1410
Arlington, Texas 76013	Group sales: 817-465-4644
UTA: 817-419-7770	

More

Too many organizations exist to allow complete coverage but the following partial list will give an idea, and telephone contact can generate more details.

Arlington Choral Society   817-460-7464

The volunteer concert choir performs a classical choral repertoire at various regional sites under director Henry Gibbons of the University of North Texas.

Arlington Symphony   817-275- 8965

Professional musicians present classical concerts. Performances at First Baptist Church.

Ballet Concerto   817-738-7915.

Local professionals present outreach programs at schools, an annual holiday performance for schoolchildren, and outdoor summer concerts.

Chamber Music Society   817-332-1610
of Fort Worth

Leading musicians from the Fort Worth-Dallas area and guest artists from around the world perform at the Texas Boys Choir's Great Hall.

Contemporary Dance/   817-922-0944
Fort Worth

A locally based professional company focuses on modern dance in performances at Orchestra Hall and elsewhere.

Fort Worth Civic Chorus   817-740-5742

Volunteer choral society presents themed concerts of classical and popular music.

Fort Worth Civic   817-346-7507
Orchestra

All-volunteer orchestra presents a series of classical concerts.

Fort Worth Classic   817-329-4430
Guitar Society

The society presents major guest artists in a subscription series at PepsiCo Recital Hall at TCU.

Fort Worth Early Music   817-923-2789

Historically authentic baroque music performed by locally based professionals at St. Andrew's Episcopal Church.

Fort Worth Men's Chorus   817-531-7546

All-male, all-volunteer choral group.

Jubilee African American   817-535-4715
Dance Ensemble

A modern dance troupe emphasizing the African-American heritage and education of young dancers.

North Texas Ballet Theatre   817-294-5731

Advanced dance students study and perform major productions with professional guest artists, including an annual presentation of *The Nutcracker.*

Renaissance Consort of   817-467-0219
Fort Worth

Director Ron Shirey conducts the 24-voice chamber choir in a variety of works at various local venues.

Southwestern Baptist Theological
Seminary Oratorio Chorus   817-923-1921

Two hundred singers from the seminary's School of Music and the community at large perform major choral works with the Fort Worth Chamber Orchestra on the campus and as resident chorus for the Fort Worth Symphony at Bass Performance Hall.

The Spectrum   817-377-0688

A locally based professional chamber ensemble that presents a series of Monday evening concerts at First United Methodist Church of Fort Worth and at First Jefferson Unitarian Universalist Church.

Texas Children's Choir   817-284-3600
3928 Diamond Loch
Fort Worth, Texas 76180

Texas Christian University   817-257-7602

Free concerts by faculty and student artists most Monday evenings at 7:30 P.M. at Ed Landreth Auditorium or the PepsiCo Recital Hall on campus. Other concerts during the school year.

Bruce Wood Dance Company   817-926-9151

Contemporary choreography, with a focus on the works of founder-director Bruce Wood, at Bass Performance Hall.

Youth Orchestra of Greater   817-923-3121
Fort Worth

Conductor Kurt Sprenger directs a comprehensive program for string players from elementary ages up and for all orchestral instruments at junior and senior high levels.

Chapter 15

Movies

Movies are better than ever. Or so "they" would have you believe. Movies may be bigger than ever, more expensive, and the special effects more spectacular. But the shows aren't always better.

Sometimes the old films *are* better than ever. That's why the Fort Worth Film Festival in *our* Sundance Square—not in Utah—is an annual event worth remembering. Chat with Michael Price, former movie critic for the *Fort Worth Star-Telegram* and now director of the Fort Worth Film Festival (www.gourmetcinema.com). See if you agree.

The 1999 Festival, second of what is to be an annual event, held October 21-24, featured screenings at the Caravan of Dreams, the Ridglea Theater, the Palace, and the Sundance 11. A few shows took place at the Black Dog Tavern and the Sage and Silo Theater.

In addition, Gregory Peck presented his two-hour one-man show at the Bass Performance Hall. Memories are made of this. There will be more to come in 2000 and—it is expected—in 2001.

A few words about ratings:

G: General Audiences. All ages admitted.
PG: Parental Guidance Suggested. Some material may not be suitable for children.

PG-13: Parents strongly cautioned. Some material may be inappropriate for children under 13.
R: Restricted. Under 17 requires accompanying parent or guardian.
NC-17: No one 17 and under admitted.
[X: Immature adults only.]

Movies are a major pastime in the good ol' U.S. of A. Here are a few places to find the latest of the motley crop.

If you know what you want to see call Moviephone: 817-444-FILM (3456) to find times, theater listings, and even reviews.

Multiplexes

Not too many years ago, a multiplex theatre had two, or three, maybe four screens in one building. Now, try to choose among ten or fifteen offerings. Tinseltown had the record with fourteen until Grapevine Mills opened with seventeen.

Most have lower prices for shows beginning before 6 P.M. During *matinee* hours, everyone gets in at child's price.

AMC Theaters

Do you still think everything's up to date in Kansas City? The International Corporate Headquarters of AMC Entertainment, Inc. keeps that Midwest city on the cutting edge.

In 1991 AMC initiated Read for the Stars, a program to encourage children under thirteen to develop reading skills. The company also takes an active fundraising role in the Big Brothers Big Sisters of America (see Chapter 11).

If your children are computer literate, the AMC website offers a game page for them.

As the organization that invented the multiplex and was first to bring multiple screen theaters to the malls of America, not to mention cup-holders in the armrests, AMC continues to lead and expand its operations worldwide. Locally, it is quite well represented.

www.amctheaters.com

Sundance Square 20

Twenty screens in two locations in downtown Fort Worth.

Sundance 11

Eleven-in-one across from the Worthington Hotel.

304 Houston Street   817-870-1111

Palace 9

Walking distance from the Worthington Hotel.

220 East Third Street   817-870-1111
Calhoun and 3rd Streets   Teleticket: 817-336-4262

Hulen 10

Ten screens in southwest Fort Worth. South of Hulen Mall for those who want to shop before—or after—the matinee. Just across the way is Lone Star Comics, with all the latest Star Wars books, action figures, and vehicles (comic books and Pokemon, too).

6330 Hulen Bend Blvd.   817-346-4994
Fort Worth, Texas

Green Oaks 8

Moving southeast, this Arlington AMC has eight theaters in one spot.

5727 I-20 at Green Oaks   817-483-0888
Arlington, Texas 76016   972-724-8000
                                   817-572 1220

Grapevine Mills 30

With stadium seating, thousands of seats, and call-ahead ticket reservations (336-4AMC), this is the largest multiplex in the Metroplex.

Highway 121 N. of I-635   972-724-8000
Grapevine, Texas

General Cinema Theaters

Operating over 1,000 screens in 24 states, General Cinema Corporation is a major player in the movie business. Especially for kids, Summer Movie Camp shows a series of family films on certain weekday mornings between June and August. Tickets for the entire series cost less than $8 per person. The theaters often sponsor special events before the movie, including such activities as face painting, coloring contests, treasure hunts, and visits from police or fire department representatives.

Theater rental for private or corporate functions can be arranged. The theater can provide the film, or you can watch your own vacation or home movies.

Gift books are available for purchase at the theaters or online through the GCC website. Extra discounts come with these purchases.

www.generalcinema.com

Arlington Park

Eight screens here.

1111 West Arbrook   817-468-8181
Arlington, Texas 76015   817-468-5243

Central Park

Eight, again.

2404 Airport Freeway   817-571-5858
Bedford, Texas 76022   817-571-7875

Ridgmar Town Square

Six screens.

6801 Ridgmar Meadow Boulevard   817-732-9388
Fort Worth, Texas 76116   817-732-7989

Loews Theaters

Now owned by the Japanese electronics giant, Loews Theaters can be found all around the country. The Sony website will tell what's playing where and give showtimes. It also allows online ticket purchase and links to other aspects of the corporate empire (music, electronics, games, and TV). Plunk a kid in front of the computer at *this* web address and you might not have to take her to a movie after all! But, just in case, here's where they are.

www.spe.sony.com/movies/

Loews City View

Six theaters.

4728 Bryant Irvin Road	817-346-4366
(Southwest) Fort Worth, Texas 76132	

Lincoln Square

Ten here.

800 Lincoln Square	817-275-7377
Collins at I-30	
Arlington, Texas 76011	

Arlington

Six more.

4930 Little Road	817-478-0977
between I-20 and Highway 287	
Arlington, Texas 76017	

United Artists Theaters

Ten theaters in the Mid-Cities just south of Highway 183.

Bedford 10

Highway 183 at Murphy	817-444-FILM
Bedford, Texas	

Bowen 8

Eight on the south side.

I-20 at Bowen   817-444-FILM

Eastchase Market 9

South of I-30 in North Arlington.

8301 Ederville Road   817-444-FILM

Fossil Creek 11

Go north toward Alliance Airport; take a break and choose from among eleven theaters.

6100 North Freeway   817-444-FILM
I-35 at Western Center Blvd

Grand Prairie 10

Ten screens.

I-20 at Carrier Parkway   817-444-FILM
Grand Prairie, Texas

Hulen 10

The ten theaters here are located just behind Hulen Mall, close enough to walk back and forth on a shopping break. Leave the car in the covered parking when that summer sun beats down.

I-20 at Hulen   817-444-FILM
Fort Worth, Texas

Las Vegas Trail 8

Eight United Artists theaters showing first-run movies.

I-30 at Las Vegas Trail   817-444-FILM
Fort Worth, Texas

MacArthur Marketplace

Opened in 1999 with sixteen huge screens, stadium seating and digital sound.

635 and MacArthur Blvd.   972-506-7170
972-444-UAUA (8282)

OMNI
Fort Worth Museum of
Science and History

Let us not forget the BIGGEST movie experience in the Metroplex! See Chapter 3 for more details.

Drive-Ins

It was rumored a few years ago that the last drive-in movie had closed (somewhere in New Jersey?), but there is still one in operation in Granbury, Texas:

The Brazos Drive-In

There are no others within driving distance of Fort Worth. One in Graham closes for the winter. The Brazos Drive-In shows current feature films Friday, Saturday, Sunday, and Monday evenings year round and still charges by the carload. Come on down! Bring the Suburban.

West Pearl Street   817-573-1311
Granbury, Texas
Admission: $13 per CARLOAD

Cheapies

Movies are not only better than ever; they're more costly than ever. Sometimes you want a bargain. Before 6 P.M., most theaters let everyone in at the child's rate. There are some opportunities for even less expense.

Short of bundling everyone into the car for a drive to the Brazos Drive-In, here are a few suggestions.

Loews

Once each year, for four weeks in October, the Loews Theaters have a special "Free Kids Film Series" at one or more of their locations. They run favorite films of the past year (a different film each week) and charge adults $1. Each adult may bring children under twelve years of age (as many as can fit in the car!) for FREE.

Wanna see a movie for a couple of bucks? Except for a possible lack of amenities and an occasional sticky floor, this is the place to take the whole gang to get more mileage from the budget:

Seventh Street Theater

For $3 per adult and $2 for a child's ticket, this is the lowest-priced regular cinematic entertainment in town. Check the seats before sitting down.

3128 West Seventh Street   817-332-6070

Chapter 16

Churches

Greater Fort Worth's Yellow Pages (SWBYP) lists thirteen pages of churches. That should give everyone a choice. Unless you're Jewish. In that case, you have to look under Synagogues (there are three).

The churches not only serve as focal points for religious activities but also, in many cases, are worth a visit for the architecture and art—such as the stained glass windows—that they display.

Though there are too many to mention each, some examples worth seeing can be found at:

First United Methodist Church
800 West Fifth Street downtown

St. Patrick's Catholic Church
1206 Throckmorton in central Fort Worth

St. Stephen Presbyterian Church
2600 Merida within view of the 1910-art deco Park Hill Bridge. This is one of the largest—if not the largest—churches in Fort Worth. Its location, a rise of the land south of Forest Park overlooking the neighborhood, makes it majestic.

Travis Avenue Baptist Church
3001 Travis Avenue/ Berry Street just west of I-35.

University Baptist Church
2720 Wabash Avenue also across from TCU

University Christian Church
2720 University Drive across from TCU

If your favorite has been overlooked, accept this apology. An entire additional volume would be required if all the churches had to be included.

Chapter 17

Seasonal Color

Color is everywhere. The nicest part about living in or visiting Texas is the change of seasons. Depending on where you are in the state, there can be two or three each year. This is different from, say, Syracuse, New York. They have two: winter and the Fourth of July.

South Texas (the Gulf Coast) has summer and hurricane season. El Paso has summer and hotter'n'Hell! Hereabouts, you find three: Summer runs from April or May to October. Fall/spring is November to January, and March to mid-April (indistinguishable except for the color of the grass). And February is either winter or rain; it varies from year to year. There's even been snow. It was back in '72, I b'lieve.

One thing doesn't change. Every season has a color. Sometimes it alters week-by-week or every month. But it's there and brighter than anywhere else in the USA.

The Texas Highway Department maintains a toll-free number for highway conditions that gives information about where the best locales for seasonal color can be found. Call 1-800-452-9292 and follow the prompts. The same number has information about highway conditions and travel warnings.

In addition, the Botanical Research Institute of Texas has a website (www.BRIT.ORG) with a link to their Metroplex Flowerwatch, which tells what's blooming where. The same

175

organization maintains a children's library with books and materials about plants and natural history.

The Oliver G. Burk Library
Botanical Research Institute of Texas

The library is open to the public from one to four in the afternoon on Tuesdays and Thursdays throughout the summer. BRIT is located in the northeast part of Downtown Fort Worth. Get to it by taking Main Street to Third. Go east on Third Street (turn right if you are facing the Courthouse) to Pecan Street. Turn right on Pecan and follow it directly into the BRIT driveway. Parking is to the left.

509 Pecan Street   817-332-4441
Fort Worth, TX 76102-4060   Metro: 817-429-3200
Fax: 817-332-4112

Autumn Leaves

Most of East Texas is a mix of evergreen and deciduous shrubbery and trees (the ones that lose their leaves in winter). Since East Texas extends to the Trinity River, it includes Fort Worth. New England and Pennsylvania are not the only places where the oaks and maples change color. For a touch of ice or snow, try Amarillo or farther up into the Panhandle. Don't stay too long up there as December and January approach with their cold and desolate weather. You may be stuck until May!

As the temperatures drop into the low forties and upper thirties, drive around the older forested neighborhoods where the maples and red oaks outnumber the live oaks (the weed that thinks it's a tree). Westover Hills, Luther Lake, Forest Park, Mistletoe Heights, and Meadows West all put on a show. The window of opportunity is narrow, however, so be alert. At least you won't have to keep tire chains in the trunk of your car as you would in Vermont.

Winter Wonderland

Texas Winter Wonderland is a little different from Yankee Country. The ground is rarely white. Maybe a little yellow while the grass rests for the spring greening. The wonder comes from the Christmas lights. Neighborhoods compete to see which can brighten the night most as the end of the year approaches.

Christmas Lights

The lights start shining right after Thanksgiving. First a few here and there, then more, 'til, finally, entire streets blaze brighter than daytime.

Certain sections of the cities have garnered a reputation for "Blessed Excess."

Interlochen (Arlington)

Cars often line up for miles to get a chance to view the lights during the weeks leading up to Christmas. If it weren't for some of the other places (see below), no one living there would be able to get home. Interlochen is located along the boundary between Arlington and Fort Worth between Village Creek and Randol Mill Parks. When the Christmas decorations go up, the adjacent villages of Tanglewood, Millbrook, and The Oaks participate in the light show. The traffic flow is heavy, so police direct cars in the area. The best way to get there is from I-30. Take the Fielder Road exit south to Randol Mill. Turn right (going west). Randol Mill becomes Westwood Drive. Follow the arrows and the other cars. Come early and remember: The lights go out at 11 P.M.

Diamond Loch

Here's another residential Christmas light show. Because it hasn't gotten as much publicity as Interlochen, the traffic is a lot lighter.

Take Denton Highway (377) south from Loop 820 or north at the split from Highway 183 in Haltom City to Glenview Drive and go east. An alternate route is *via* Grapevine Highway (26) and west at Glenview.

Turn East on Devonshire and right (south) on Diamond Loch. Follow Diamond Loch as it crosses Glenview to make a sparkling circle. Follow it to the right and return to the entrance.

There are several turns onto side streets, which will allow you to see more lights, but each ends in a cul-de-sac, and you will have to turn back to Diamond Loch.

Westover Hills

From I-30 going west out of downtown, exit at Camp Bowie Boulevard but keep in the right lane and go north on Horne Street. Just beyond Bryce look for Westover Hills to your left. Enter on Westover Drive and enjoy the sights. Don't behave in a suspicious manner. Westover Hills has its own police force, which is diligent about guarding this well-to-do neighborhood.

Luther Lake

Bounded by Clayton Road, Brants Lane, and Rowan Drive, this tiny puddle is surrounded by homes whose owners decorate their property along the lakefront. Clayton Road bridges a creek (one of the numerous tributaries of the Trinity) at the eastern end of the lake. From this vantage the lights reflect in the water, giving a cheery glow to winter nights.

Meadows West

This southwest Fort Worth neighborhood rivals Interlochen's Christmas light show. Take Bryant Irvin Road north from I-20 to Bellaire Drive South. Turn left and drive 1.8 miles to Meadows West. Cruise around the many streets and try to guess which has the most lights. The task will be difficult.

Mont Del Estates

Backtrack from Meadows West along Bellaire Drive South to Legend Road. Take Legend (you can only turn one way) to Crosslands Road and turn right into Mont Del. The lights will lead you. Mont Del Estates is perched on a hill in Benbrook. From certain points it is possible to see the lights of downtown Fort Worth. Tandy Center's twin towers become giant candles at Christmastime.

Flowers Fantastic

Lady Bird Johnson's enduring influence on the Lone Star State is visible along the highways and byways throughout the spring, summer, and autumn. Don't forget that in *this* state, spring starts in March and summer lasts until October.

Spring Azaleas

Take a drive through the Botanic Gardens in the first days of spring. Or go to Dallas and circle Turtle Creek (look for the hole in the creek!) or Samuell Grand Park. The Azaleas burst forth all at once with glowing reds robing shrubbery that had been first leafless and then darkly green with new foliage. Suddenly all is bright, the varied shades blending one into the next. Capture the color in your camera with Fuji film. It makes the reds leap out of the image.

April Bluebonnets

The photo opportunity sought by every parent of a toddler comes each year with the lupine flowers. The fields of blue and white sprout tripod-mounted cameras focused on babies plunked in the midst. Red feathers of Indian paintbrush accent the scenery. A few of the best places to find and photograph the bluebonnets are:

The Benbrook traffic circle at the conjunction of Camp Bowie Boulevard, Highway 183, and Highway 377.

Highway 377 south of the Benbrook Circle. Look on the west side of 377 north of I-20.

Jacksboro Highway (Highway 199) north from Loop 820 toward Azle.

Interstate-30 between Fort Worth and Arlington.

Legend Road (south side) between Crosslands Road and Bellaire Drive S. in Benbrook.

Wildflowers Galore!

Wildflowers sprinkle color around the fields and roadsides starting early in the spring. Peaking when the royal bluebonnets blanket the land with white-capped cerulean, the parade of pigment persists all summer and well into the fall. Indian paintbrush accents the blue mantle with red flames. Even after the state flowers have gone to seed, oxeye daisies, phlox, gaillardia, sunflowers, and Mexican hats keep the colors glowing through the summer and fall. Pastel primroses and yellow coreopsis set off the brilliant red of the fruit of prickly pear, or the multicolored flowers of claret cup, prickly pear, and lace cactus.

Hundreds of species of amazing wildflowers bloom throughout the year in Texas. Each season has a special breed. Every part of the Lone Star State is distinctive. How can you tell which is which and where you are? Take a day trip to Austin (see Chapter 17):

Lady Bird Johnson Wildflower Center

Lady Bird's legacy spreads from Austin in all directions. The National Wildflower Research Center, renamed in her honor, claims as its mission the role of "educating people about the environmental necessity, economic value, and natural beauty of native plants."

The Center showcases more than 400 species of grasses, trees, shrubs, and wildflowers native to Central Texas. Of perhaps greater importance, it also serves the entire nation as an educational resource for gardening with and restoration of regional native plants.

You may rent the facility for private functions (such as weddings) after hours or on Mondays, when it is normally closed.

How to get there: Take I-35 through Austin to Exit 227 (Slaughter Lane). Follow Slaughter Lane west to Loop 1 (MOPAC). Turn left (south) and take the first left on La Crosse. The Center will be on the right.

4801 La Crosse Avenue   512-292-4200
Austin, Texas 78739   512-292-4100
www.wildflower.org   FAX: 512-292-4627
Hours: Every Day during April
Remainder of the year:
Grounds
Tuesday-Sunday 9 A.M.-5:30 P.M.
Visitors Gallery
Tuesday-Saturday 9 A.M.-4 P.M., Sunday, 1-4 P.M.
Wild Ideas: The New Store
Tuesday-Saturday 9 A.M.-5:30 P.M., Sunday 1-4 P.M.
The Wildflower Cafe
Tuesday-Saturday 9 A.M.-4 P.M., Sunday 11 A.M.-4 P.M.
The Little House
Saturday 10 A.M.-noon, 1-4 P.M., Sunday 1-4 P.M.
Entrance Fees:

Wildflower Center Members Free
Adults $4, Students and Senior Citizens $2.50
Children 4 years and under Free
Tours and group rates available with advance reservation.

Fireworks

From late June until the middle of July no excuse is necessary to set off fireworks. All because of Independence Day. Benbrook Summerfest during the last weekend in June is usually the first occasion. Fireworks glow over Benbrook Lake, reflecting starbursts in the water.

When July 4th arrives, every city in the region produces a pyrotechnic exhibit. Fort Worth lights up the sky above the Trinity on the night of the Fourth and, in the east, Dallas does the same.

Local newspapers list locations and hours for the displays. Sometimes, when the weather has been uncooperative and draught conditions prevail, the fireworks may be canceled or postponed.

Chapter 18

Dining

Although no vacation is complete without food, sometimes just going out to eat can be a vacation for Mom. Too many eating establishments exist to attempt even a minimally comprehensive list, but these are a few of my favorites. Restaurants come and go, occasionally without warning, so call ahead to be sure the one you choose is open and still at the same address. No attempt has been made to include *every* possibility, so don't worry if your top choice is missing. Write the author and maybe it can be added to the next edition.

Breakfast

The most important meal of the day. And the following are a few of the reasons.

Paris Coffee Shop

A Fort Worth institution for more than fifty years, this is *the* place for biscuits and cream gravy. Traditional cowboy fare is unsurpassed for breakfast and lunch, and the Sunday brunch will leave you breathless if you try to eat it all.

700 West Magnolia Avenue
Fort Worth, Texas 76104

817-335-2041
FAX: 817-335-9525

Cactus Flower

Another spot for that famous biscuits-and-gravy or eggs and all the alternatives, it is also renowned for the biggest, sweetest, stickiest cinnamon buns in America.

509 University
Fort Worth, Texas 76107
817-332-9552

2401 Westport Parkway
(Near Alliance Airport)
Fort Worth, Texas 76177
817-491-9524

Burdav's

And another! Eggs as you like 'em with biscuits *and* grits (or hash browns for those less true Southerners)!

4120 West Vickery Boulevard
Fort Worth, Texas 76107

817-737-2277

Dixie Café

Not only breakfast, but lunch and supper, too. Chicken fried steak the way it's supposed to taste.

4902 Highway 377 S.
Benbrook, Texas 76116
Hours: Monday-Saturday, 6 A.M.-9 P.M., Sunday, 7 A.M.-4 P.M.

817-244-4421

Don't Forget Denny's and IHOP

Found all over town. Check the Yellow Page listings. Or keep your eyes open; sometimes they appear out of nowhere.

Brunch

Kind of an institution in the American South, this meal is neither breakfast nor lunch but a blending of the two into a *gourmandizing gobblefest*. In most places, once or twice a year will satisfy your hunger for days or longer. That is certainly true for our first entrant:

Sunday at the Worthington

Bring an appetite, wear loose clothing, and plan to stay awhile. This is the meal that defines brunch. Every breakfast food imaginable followed by all the luncheon entrees this five-star hotel's chefs can conjure.

This is a champagne brunch, served every Sunday of the year from 10 A.M. to 2 P.M. The last seating is at 1:30. Reservations are recommended, but not required.

200 Main Street   817-870-1000
Fort Worth, Texas 76102
$29.95, Chldren 5-12 $10.95, Under 5 Free

Sundance Deli

(See below.)

Cafeterias

Cafeterias provide comfortable, economical spots all around the town for family meals with that home-cooked style. Yellow Page listings give addresses and phone numbers. Call ahead for hours, specials, and to find out how busy they are.

Luby's

With fifteen locations, Luby's leads the pack. One is bound to be nearby.

Colonial

Two more to fill in geographic gaps.

Furr's

Furr's has four sites: Euless, Arlington, North Richland Hills, and one in Fort Worth.

Hamburgers
The All-American Food!

Here are the best the West has to offer. Ground beef never tasted so good.

Kincaid's

Arguably serving the best hamburger in Fort Worth, if not Texas, this place started out as a grocery store and has been run by members of the founding family since 1946. Tables have replaced shelves and stand-up counters added, making dine-in or take-home versions of the tastiest, just-right burgers available in the Metroplex.

4901 Camp Bowie Boulevard	817-732-2881
Fort Worth, Texas 76107	FAX: 817-731-3278
Hours: Monday-Saturday 11 A.M.-6 P.M.	

Charley's

Serving from two locations, this is definitely the top runner-up to Kincaid's. *Al fresco* dining and delivery are both acceptable options.

3620 Alta Mere	817-244-5223
4616 Granbury Road	817-924-8611

Tommy's

In third place, but still way ahead of the Golden Arches, Tommy's has three locations for table dining or take-out and a downtown site at 400 Houston Street (817-334-0999).

140 East Exchange	817-625-6654
2701 Green Oaks Road	817-735-9651
7028 Navajo Trail	817-237-9992

Cypress Café

A new kid on the block, but well worth the trip. Cypress Café opened its doors at Cityview Center in 1999 with unpretentious ambience and a limited menu. The burgers, made only with fresh beef, easily rival Kincaid's and Charley's. There may be a new number one by the turn of the century. Hint: try the 1/3 pound version. It will be plenty for most appetites (only linebackers in training will need the 1/2 pounder). And be sure to get some onion rings, made with real onion!

4750 Bryant Irvin Road817-370-9888
Cityview Center
Fort Worth, Texas 76132

Other burger joints include **Chapp's** (with locations in southwest Fort Worth and Arlington) and **Leta's Grill** in the Stockyards area.

Fast Food Chains

Big Macs, Whoppers, Jumbo Jacks. You name it; we got it in Fort Worth. Taco Bell, Bueno, or Cabana. Likewise. Go to any major intersection and throw a rock. Chances are, it'll hit one of those drive-through menu thingies.

If you believe the best surprise is no surprise except for the plastic Star Wars prize in your Happy Meal, you'll have no trouble enjoying lunch here.

Boston Market, KFC, Pizza Hut/Inn, Chili's, Bennigan's. We got 'em all. All good. All the same as everywhere else.

Sandwiches, etc.

TGIFriday

Hard to believe TGIFriday turned thirty-four years old in 1999. Although it all began as a way for its founder, an unmarried former perfume executive, to meet stewardesses (that's what flight attendants were called way back then) TGIFriday has become a family-friendly place to dine. It boasts one of the best kid's menus in the chain restaurant business and serves generous portions at reasonable prices. Numerous locations around the Metroplex assure accessibility. They even have two in D/FW airport (at Terminal 2E, near gate 12 and Terminal 4E, near gate 16).

Locations west of Dallas

6851-C Green Oaks Road, Fort Worth	817-735-8184
4646 Southwest Loop 820, Fort Worth	817-738-3335
1000 Ballpark Way, Suite 401, Arlington	817-265-5191
1041 Highway 114 West, Grapevine	817-421-8443
2505 S. Stemmons Freeway, Lewisville	972-315-1622
1524 N. Collins, Arlington	817-261-2390
8605 Airport Freeway, N. Richland Hills	817-788-2451
4601 S. Cooper, Arlington	817-467-1349

The Lunch Box

Tucked away in the 6333 shopping strip, this *petite* tearoom may take a little hunting to find. It's worth the effort; a great place for moms and dads and daughters and sons (choose your own combination). Soup, salad, and excellent sandwiches. A nice, lite lunch for any appetite.

6333 Camp Bowie Boulevard   817-738-2181
Fort Worth, Texas 76116
Monday-Saturday, 11-3

Sundance Market and Deli

A cross between an upscale gourmet grocery and a comfortable cafeteria, this is where the downtown worker breaks fast before starting the workday. The lunch crowd can select specialty items to take home for the evening meal. On Friday and Saturday, the former owners of Harper's Bluebonnet Bakery keep this place open 'til eleven. And it sets one of the best brunch tables in the area from 9 A.M. to 3 P.M. every Sunday.

353 Throckmorton Street   817-335-DELI(3354)
Fort Worth, Texas 76102

White Eagle Deli

The place to go for some of the best and most reasonably priced sandwiches in the city. Once you find the White Eagle, you'll always come back. Even if only for a snack or lunch for yourself. Their sandwich trays can feed a small army.

1560 N. Sylvania Ave.   817-838-3821
Fort Worth, Texas 76111

Jason's Deli

Multiple locations

New York style with Texas generosity. A ten-gallon appetite
is needed to finish one of their sandwiches.

Carshon's

Fort Worth's ONLY genuine Kosher-style deli. Corned beef
and pastrami just like on Broadway in the Big Apple. Pie to
die for. And, of course, bagels.

3133 Cleburne Road   817-923-1907
Fort Worth, Texas 76110

Pizza

Domino's, Pappa John's, Pizza Hut, and the other chain fran-
chises can be found all over town. Call for free delivery.
When food alone isn't enough, try:

Chuck E. Cheese's

With multiple spots around the Metroplex, this really is the
place "where a kid can be a kid." And the parents can, too!
Games and pizza. What more could a kid ask. Locations in
D/FW:

Arlington	3200 Justiss Dr.	817-649-2933
	2216 Fielder Rd.	817-861-1561
Dallas	13125 Montfort	972-392-1944
	7110 S. Westmoreland	972-298-7973
Fort Worth	7935 Grapevine Hwy.	817-281-4600
Garland	1340 W. Centerville Rd.	972-681-1385
Irving	3903 W. Airport Frwy.	972-256-1600
Lewisville	(across from Vista	972-315-6260
	Ridge Mall)	
Plano	1604 Preston Road	972-599-0512
Richardson	1235 E. Beltline Rd.	972-234-8778

White 7750 Scott Street 817-367-0084
Settlement
Check their websites for coupon offers:
www.chuckecheese.com and www.coolsavings.com/cec.

Joe's Pizza Pasta and Subs

Pizza by the slice; pizza by the pie. Pasta dishes to ease all hunger pangs. And, affordable. There are twenty or more Joe's around the Metroplex. Unpretentious—that means "no ambience"—but you may dine there or carry out and feast at home without destroying the budget.

4407 Little Road	4750 Bryant Irvin Road
Arlington, Texas	Fort Worth, Texas 76132
817-483-0200	817-263-1133

Tex-Mex

Joe T. Garcia's

No visit to Fort Worth can be considered complete without a stop at this landmark. Come for the atmosphere, but be sure to enjoy the food. The restaurant that began as a tiny house has grown, amoeba-like, to encompass open-air gardens, multiple dining rooms, and party facilities.

2140 North Commerce Street 817-626-4356
Fort Worth, Texas 76106 817-429-5166
817-624-0266

Dixie Café

It is difficult to determine where to classify this unimposing roadside eatery. The menu is varied and goes from breakfast to dinner with a broad range of styles, all remarkably good. The Mexican cuisine, however, puts them on the map! Their skill travels well, so if you need a party catered, don't hesitate to call.

4902 Highway 377 S   817-244-4421
Benbrook, Texas 76116
Monday-Saturday, 6 A.M.-9 P.M., Sunday, 7 A.M.-3 P.M.

Uncle Julio's

For a chain restaurant, Uncle Julio's has a singular atmosphere. A Mexican Sunday brunch here is a memorable experience. They will cater your private party—in the party room or at your chosen location—to set a special south-of-the-border mood. Call 817-244-7697 for more information.

5301 Camp Bowie Boulevard   817-377-2777
Fort Worth, Texas 76107

Don Pablo's

A chain, but a good one serving limitless chips and salsa before and during the meal.

Other Mexican restaurant chains are represented in Fort Worth—Pulidos and El Fenix, to name a couple—but space constraints won't permit listing all. Papa Pedro Pulido died at the age of ninety-one on July 31, 1999. He and his wife Donicia opened their first restaurant in 1966. It is still open on Pulido Street west of University Drive in Fort Worth. The Pulido family is actively involved in the operation of the restaurant chain.

Fort Worth:
5601 S. Hulen   7050 Ridgmar Meadow Road
817-346-3887   817-731-0497

Grapevine:
1709 Crossroads Drive
817-421-2981

Steak

This is Texas, after all, and beef is what's for dinner. Steak is a staple of the diet here, and the places that serve it range from the magnificent **Del Frisco's Double Eagle Steak House** to the sublime **Outback Steakhouse** (*another* chain!). **Reata**, atop the Bank One building serves it southwestern style accompanied by a view of the city.

But the place to take the family is:

Williams Ranch House

Today's best tastes—ribeyes, brisket, chicken-fried steak—with an air of the seventies. Prices, too.

5532 Jacksboro Highway   817-624-1272
Fort Worth, Texas 76114
Hours: Wednesday-Monday, 5-10 P.M.

Or

River Oaks Steak House

Used to be a Bonanza and the atmosphere's the same. But the beef is good and the prices are right for family dining on a budget.

4335 River Oaks Boulevard   817-626-8866
Fort Worth, Texas 76114
Hours: Sunday-Thursday, 11 A.M.-9 P.M.
Friday-Saturday, 11 A.M.-10 P.M.

Italian

Who *doesn't* like spaghetti? Or ravioli? Or pizza? The Spaghetti Warehouse and Romano's Macaroni Grill have proven America still loves pasta. Home cookin' still can't be topped, and the best homemade Italian comes from one of two places in Fort Worth. Family dining is the way to go at Mancuso's. For intimate *tete-a-tete* choose On Broadway where they have to push tables together to seat groups larger than four. Food's great either place.

Mancuso's

Cathy Mancuso owns and operates the BEST Italian restaurant in Fort Worth. And she does the cooking, just like Mama used to do, so you know it'll be good.

Try the fried mozzarella for an appetizer. Like fish? The Italian fish platter is enough for two hearty appetites. And the pizza is the cheesiest in the world. Sample the pesto pizza for something different.

9500 White Settlement Road   817-246-7041
Fort Worth, Texas 76108

On Broadway

Another fine spot for pasta, excellent salads, and continental specialties, On Broadway is a family-run restaurant that has been around for a long time in the same location. That speaks volumes in this business. Veal Romano and grilled salmon are unsurpassed. Don't pass up the garlic bread. Or the dessert!

6306 Hulen Bend Boulevard   817-346-8841
Fort Worth, Texas 76132

Sardine's

One more good place for garlic bread and oregano. Almost directly opposite the Amon Carter Museum, this dark cavern provides a tasty way to end a day of museum-hopping or to start off an evening at the Scott Theater. Come early to avoid a wait. Sidewalk tables make outdoor dining an option before the summer heat sets in.

Bella Italia West

Where do you go for something a bit out of the ordinary? Here's an Italian restaurant that specializes in wild game. Want your pasta with emu or ostrich? Antelope or venison? How about buffalo or quail? This is the place.

5139 Camp Bowie Blvd   817-738-1700
Fort Worth, Texas 76107   FAX: 817-738-1784

Prima Pasta

A fun family place for all kinds of pasta dishes. Bring your own wine.

6108 South Hulen   817-263-7711
Fort Worth, Texas 76132

Chinese

Here, there, and everywhere, Oriental restaurants pop up like Fortune cookies. Outside New York or San Francisco, it is difficult to find any that truly excel. Fort Worth has one or two.

Szechuan

The best choice. Try it and see. Other locations on Locke and Grapevine Highway are not *quite* as good.

4750 Bryant Irvin Road   817-346-6111
Cityview Center
Fort Worth, Texas 76132

B KK Narita

Featuring a variety of Oriental cuisines (Chinese, Japanese, Thai), the menu here is enticing and has something for every taste.

6060 Southwest Boulevard   817-738-3175
Fort Worth, Texas 76109

Barbecue

This is Texas, after all, and you're probably wondering why it has taken so long to get to this topic. Saving the best for last? Not really. Barbecue—or Bar-B-Q, or however you spell it—comes in so many forms that we can't narrow the field. To purists, barbecue has to be pork. But in Fort Worth, brisket rules!

Ribs, however, must also be available. All the best places have both, as well as chicken. The main problem is deciding *which* to select. Like your B-B-Q Memphis-style? Try **Red Hot And Blue** or **Tony Roma's**. Prefer down-home Texas brisket? **The Railhead** or **The Galleries** should keep you happy. Want it smoked on the spot? Even though it is a chain, **Colter's** does great ribs and chicken. And, since we're on the subject, a ride to Dallas for the **Original Sonny Bryan's** might be in order, too.

Angelo's

The Fort Worth landmark revered by Stock Show attendees, Angelo's is the old-time, sawdust-on-the-floor, picnic table and pitcher-of-beer, cowboy barbecue. This may not be the place for little ones, but the food'll travel and the memories will remain.

2533 White Settlement   817-332-0357
Fort Worth, Texas 76107

Cousins

A new location opened in October 1999. Dine inside or on the *al fresco* patio or take it home in any quantity you can carry. There's beef, pork, ribs, sausage, and chicken—never forget the chicken. Cousin's has the juiciest, tastiest chicken in the country.

The original site still serves the same stuff.

5125 Bryant Irvin Road   6262 McCart Avenue

Fort Worth, Texas 76132
817-346-3999
1-888-BRISKET (274-7538)
FAX: 817-3463771

Fort Worth, Texas 76133
817-346-2511

The Galleries

In spite of the somewhat "seedy" nature of the neighborhood, the food is worth the trip. Best for lunch in the light of day or to order for take-out.

Jerry's

Top-notch catered barbecue comes from Jerry's, but they serve in-house, too, and the new one in Fort Worth has the same good stuff! Thomas "Stretch" Reed brings the food from Aledo. He runs the Fort Worth location and claims there has been no sign of hungry dogs following the truck.

100 S. Front Street
Aledo, Texas 76008
817-441-5900

2929 University
Fort Worth, Texas 76107
817-878-2500

Seafood

Fresh fish, fresh-caught and freshly prepared, is harder to find this far inland than bean burritos. These are the top choices:

Bill and Marty Martin's Famous Seafood Restaurant

The short drive south on I-35 is worth the reward at the other end. We liked it better when it was in town, but the food is the same as ever.

Get off at Bethesda Road(Exit 32) and cross under the highway. Then go north on the frontage road. Come early. They don't take reservations.

2701 South I-35W
Fort Worth, Texas 76028

817-447-1277

Harbor One

Another trip, this time north towards Eagle Mountain Lake, again provides gustatory piscine pleasure.

9315 Boat Club Road   817-236-7449
Fort Worth, Texas 76179

The Water Street Seafood Company

One more spot to find the fruits of the watery realm. Close to the museums and the Zoo, Botanic Garden, and Log Cabin Village.

1540 S. University Drive   817-877-3474
Fort Worth, Texas 76107

Texas Grill

Down home cookin' since 1988 at either location, but the best fried catfish in the area is at the Benbrook address.

Camp Bowie Boulevard   9413 Highway 377 S.
Fort Worth, Texas 76116   Benbrook, Texas 76126
817-377-0270   817-249-1158

Bagels

It now seems there's a bagel place on every corner. Real New York bagels cannot be obtained in the Metroplex. Find the closest approximation at **Bagelstein's** on Spring Valley Road at Coit in Dallas. In Fort Worth, you'll have to settle for either **Yogi's** or **Einstein Bros**. Others, with their own special quality, include:

Benny's

165 Harwood Road   817-285-7136
Fort Worth, Texas 76054

Bruegger's

6405 N. Beach   817-306-0770

5837 Camp Bowie	817-377-1276
420 Grapevine Highway	817-427-1128
2315 E. Southlake Boulevard	817-421-9553

Einstein Bros.

3050 S. University	817-923-3444
1827 SW Green Oaks Boulevard	817-419-0488
2200 Airport Freeway	817-354-5773

Carshon's

(see under Sandwiches, above)

Yogi's Bagel Cafe

Breakfast omelets, grilled sandwiches, and bagels, bagels, bagels! Get 'em to go or eat café-style inside or out front, *al fresco*.

| 2710 S. Hulen | 817-921-4500 |
| Fort Worth, Texas 76109 | |

Ice Cream

Now, everyone in Texas knows there's no finer ice cream than Blue Bell. The best way to eat it is in large quantities, and the best place is at the Creamery in Brenham. New Yorkers have been known to pay exorbitant prices to get Blue Bell shipped to the Big Apple. And we can buy it at any grocery store! How lucky are Texans?

Sometimes, however, the urge to watch someone else scoop the confection into cups, cones, or dishes is almost overwhelming, and we let our sweet teeth get the better of us. When that happens, the old-fashioned ice cream parlor is the haven sought. Don't forget frozen yogurt (**TCBY**), **Sno Cones**, and **Dairy Queen**, all at numerous locations.

Marble Slab Creamery

These and four other locations in the area serve it plain or sprinkled with any topping you can imagine.

3930 Glade Road	817-267-3236
312-A Houston Street	817-335-5877
5427 S. Hulen	817-370-0054
2201 W. Southlake Boulevard #123	817-329-8309

The Back Porch

In the heart of the museum district, food can be had, but the ice cream is the reason to come after theater or Stock Show.

3400-B Camp Bowie	817-332-1422
Fort Worth, Texas 76107	

Braum's

All around the town, banana splits, and sundaes piled high with whipped cream, nuts, and cherries. There are twenty or more Braum's Ice Cream and Dairy stores in the Fort Worth area. Check the Yellow Pages.

Still hungry?

Here's space to make notes of some of your own favorites.

Chapter 19

When Something Unexpected Happens

When you live or travel with children, the only certainty is uncertainty.

So, when something out of the ordinary occurs, what next? First, don't panic. Then, seek the appropriate assistance. Here are some choices.

Emergencies

Like all major cities in the United States, Fort Worth has the 911 system. This is for fire, police, and ambulance. The caller's number is automatically displayed at the answering center to enable more rapid response. The display remains, even if the connection is broken.

Remember to teach the youngsters when NOT to use 911.

Some cities (Dallas is one) also have 311 for less urgent problems, but that system is not yet available in Fort Worth as this book goes to press. Nonemergency telephone numbers for the area are listed below.

Poisoning

1-800-POISON1 (764-7661)
North Texas Poison Center: 1-800-441-0040

In the case of poisoning or *suspected* poisoning go to the nearest hospital emergency room. If possible, bring along the container of the toxic agent and try to estimate how much was taken.

Children's Emergency

Call 817-885-4093 to get emergency advice when a child is ill or injured.

FBI

817-336-7135
If no answer: (Dallas) 214-720-2200

Hopefully, you'll never need this number, but isn't it reassuring to know they might *NOT* answer?

U.S. Secret Service

972-868-3200 (Dallas)

You shouldn't need this one, either.

National Youth Crisis Hotline

1-800-442-4673

Nonemergency Telephone Numbers:

Locality	Police	Fire
Argyle	940-464-7254	940-240-3840
Arlington	817-459-5700	817-459-5500
Azle	817-444-3221	817-444-3221
Bedford	817-952-2121	817-952-2121
Benbrook	817-249-2752	817-249-1727
Blue Mound	817-232-0661	817-232-0661
Burleson	817-295-7146	817-295-5498
Colleyville	817-281-5007	817-488-6227
Crowley	817-297-2276	817-297-1638
Dalworthington Gardens	817-275-1234	817-275-1234
Dido	817-884-1212	817-232-9800

Locality	Police	Fire
Double Oaks	817-898-5600	817-430-0013
Eagle Mountain Lake	817-884-1212	817-236-8044
Edgecliff	817-884-1212	817-293-4317
Euless	817-685-1500	817-685-1600
Everman	817-293-2937	817-293-6870
Forest Hill	817-531-5250	817-531-1043
Fort Worth	817-335-4222	817-922-3000
Haltom City	817-222-7000	817-834-7321
Haslet	817-884-1212	
Hurst	817-788-7146	817-788-7183
Keller	817-431-1515	817-431-3371
Kennedale	817-478-5416	817-478-5322
Lakeside	817-237-1234	817-237-7461
Lake Worth	817-237-1224	817-237-7461
Mansfield	817-473-9381	817-473-1104
North Richland Hills	817-581-5550	817-581-5670
Pantego	817-274-1383	817-274-1384
Pelican Bay	817-444-3221	
Rendon	817-884-1212	817-478-0221
Richland Hills	817-595-6612	817-595-6635
River Oaks	817-626-1991	817-626-3786
Roanoke	817-491-6052	817-491-2301
Saginaw	817-232-0311	817-232-4640
Sansom Park	817-626-1921	817-626-1921
Southlake	817-481-5581	817-481-5581
Spillway	817-884-1212	817-237-6369
Watauga	817-281-3307	817-281-3307
Westover Hills	817-737-3127	817-922-3127
Westworth Village	817-738-3694	817-738-3694
White Settlement	817-246-7070	817-246-1761

Other Fort Worth Nonemergency Numbers:

Sheriff	817-884-1212
Ambulance	817-922-3150
Texas Department of Public Safety	
Northwest (Lake Worth)	817-238-9197
South	817-294-1075
Regional Office (Garland)	817-226-7611

Need a Doctor?

Newcomers to the area—or to parenthood—sometimes must find a physician in a hurry. This, of course, is the worst time to need one. It usually results in an unnecessary, frequently expensive trip to the hospital emergency room. Ideally, one should have a doctor (pediatrician) selected prior to birth of the first child. But, what does one do when new to the city?

Numerous physician and dentist referral services will give names and office addresses of several members whose offices are close to home or workplaces. Some will even make the connection or schedule appointments. It is wise to remember that participants in these services frequently pay a fee to get the referrals. While this does not mean that they are not qualified, it does mean that the referral services are not entirely unbiased. Those that do not charge the doctor a fee are hospital-run and only refer patients to members of the hospital staff.

The best way to choose a physician is to get a reference from a friend or neighbor and see the doctor in person to learn if your personalities "mesh." And don't be shy about asking to know the doctor's qualifications (board certification, medical society membership, and specialty training). No reputable physician or dentist should be reluctant to disclose this information to a prospective patient.

Some of the referral services are:

Tarrant County Medical Society	817-732-2825
TCMS Arlington Branch	817-732-3997
Tarrant County Academy of Family Physicians	817-249-2940
Carelink (Osteopathic Health System of Texas)	817-654-2344
Carelink (Osteopathic Medical Center)	817-735-3627
Helpline (Baylor Grapevine)	1-800-422-9567
Plaza Medical Center of Fort Worth	1-800-265-8624
Harris Wellcare	817-654-9355
1-800-DOCTORS	1-800-362-8677

When someone's sick

Unexpected illness is an oxymoron. When it happens at home there is usually a plan. But what about when it disrupts a vacation? In a large city, the choices are many and often confusing. Fort Worth is fortunate to have numerous excellent hospitals and a variety of urgent care facilities with extended hours.

Hospitals

These are all listed in the Yellow Pages but are noted here for quick reference:

Cook Children's Medical Center
801 Seventh Avenue   817-885-4000
Fort Worth, Texas 76104-2796   www.cookchildrens.org

All Saints Episcopal Hospital and All Saints Cityview
1400 Eighth Avenue   7100 Oakmont Blvd.
Fort Worth, Texas 76104   Fort Worth, Texas 76132
817-926-2544   817-346-5700
www.allsaints.com

Baylor Medical Center   www.baylorhealth.com
Grapevine   **Irving**
1650 W. College Street   1901 N. MacArthur Blvd.
Grapevine, Texas 76051   Irving, Texas 75061
817-481-1588   972-579-8100

Plaza Medical Center
900 Eighth Avenue   817-336-2100
Fort Worth, Texas 76104   www.columbia.net

North Hills Medical Center
4401 Booth Calloway Road   817-590-1000
North Richland Hills, Texas 76180
www.columbia.net

Medical Center of Arlington
3301 Matlock Road   817-465-3241
Arlington, Texas 76015   www.columbia-hca.com
www.columbia.net

John Peter Smith Hospital
1500 South Main Street   817-921-3431
Fort Worth, Texas 76104   Metro: 429-5156
www.jpshealthnet.org

Osteopathic Medical Center of Texas
1000 Montgomery Street   817-731-4311
Fort Worth, Texas 76107   www.ohst.com

Arlington Memorial Hospital
800 West Randol Mill Road   817-548-6100
Arlington, Texas 76012

Harris Methodist   www.hmhs.com
   Fort Worth   817-882-2000
   1301 Pennsylvania Avenue
   Fort Worth, Texas 76104

   Southwest   817-346-5000
   6100 Harris Parkway
   Fort Worth, Texas 76132

   Northwest   817-444-8600
   108 Denver Trail
   Azle, Texas 76020

   HEB   817-685-4000
   1600 Hospital Parkway
   Bedford, Texas 76022

Huguley Memorial Medical Center
11801 South Freeway   817-293-9110
Fort Worth, Texas 76115   www.ahss.org

Urgent Care Centers

Nearly every strip mall has a walk-in clinic with extended
hours (usually 8 A.M. to 9 or 10 P.M.) where routine health
care is available and minor emergencies can be treated.
Most will take local insurance plans for payment. All accept
various credit cards and even—can you believe it?—cash.
There are chains in Dallas and Fort Worth called PrimaCare
(separate business entities in each county using the same

name) with clinics at numerous locations. In Dallas County they close at 9 P.M., although some have different hours of operation. Those in Tarrant County stay open until 10 P.M. They can handle most minor emergency problems and arrange for referral of more complicated cases. However if you know you have a serious emergency, it is faster to go directly to the nearest hospital.

In Arlington, Dr. John Hood provides walk-in medical clinic services from 8 A.M.-7 P.M. Monday, Tuesday, Thursday, and Friday, and from 8-2 P.M. Wednesday and Saturday. His office is at 6201 Matlock. The phone number is 817-467- 7373 or (817-472-8200).

PrimaCare Medical Centers

Fort Worth   817-294-1651
6404 McCart (near Alta Mesa)
Fort Worth, Texas 76133

Eastchase   817-459-2005
1661 Eastchase Parkway at I-30
Fort Worth, Texas 76120

Fossil Creek   817-514-8668
6340 North Beach Street (at Western Center)
Fort Worth, Texas 76137

Arlington   817-465-4928
3295 South Cooper (at Mayfield)
Arlington, Texas 76015

Hurst   817-428-7300
400 Mid Cities Boulevard
Highway 26 and Cheek-Sparger
Hurst, Texas 76054

Duncanville   972-780-0802
726 Cockerell Hill Road
Duncanville, Texas 75137

Grand Prairie   972-264-5858
3950 South Carrier Parkway, Suite 110
Grand Prairie, Texas 75052

Bedford-Euless   817-251-2101
5301 William D Tate
Grapevine, Texas 76051

Grapevine Mills   972-539-6330
2355 Grapevine Mills Circle East
Grapevine, Texas 76051
Hours: Monday-Friday 8 A.M.-10 P.M.
Saturday 8 A.M.-8 P.M., Sunday 10 A.M.-6 P.M.

Tarrant County Medical Society

Academy of Medicine

New residents can get help finding a doctor from the County Medical Society. A selection of physician members' names, office addresses, and telephone numbers specific to geographical region (by ZIP code) is available free of charge by calling them.

The county medical society can only give numbers for physicians who are members. Although most M.D.s (doctor of medicine) and many D.O.s (doctor of osteopathic medicine) belong, not all do. There are excellent physicians in both of these very similar branches of medicine.

3850 Tulsa Way   817-732-2825
Fort Worth, TX 76107   FAX: 817-732-3033
www.tcms.org

Fort Worth District Dental Society

Don't forget their teeth! This list is current as we go to press. Newcomers to the professional community may not yet be listed.

6145 Wedgwood Drive   817-263-7176
Fort Worth, TX 76133
Hours: Monday-Thursday, 8 A.M.-4 P.M.

Dentists specializing in children

Bruce Weiner, D.D.S
6210 John Ryan Drive
Fort Worth, TX 76132

817-292-5140
FAX: 817-292-3842

D. Gordon Strole Jr.
3550 Hulen-C Street
Fort Worth, Texas 76107-6812
E-mail: dgs@fastlane.net

817-732-9341
FAX: 817-732-7021

Harry M. Stimmel
3050 Sycamore School Road
Fort Worth, Texas 76133-7771

817-370-0021

Susan M. Roberts-Geddes
6650 North Beach, #118
Fort Worth, Texas 76137

817-656-3999
FAX: 817-656-7862

David L. Purczinsky
6304 Walburn Court
Fort Worth, Texas 76133

817-625-6895
FAX: 817-625-6882

George Stanley Preece
3537 West Seventh Street
Fort Worth, Texas 76107
E-mail: kpreece@metronet.com

817-737-3141
FAX: 817-377-8970

Jack W. Morrow
1533 Merrimac Circle, #209
Fort Worth, Texas 76107

817-332-9835
FAX: 817-336-8733

Bridget D. McAnthony
1124 S. Lake Street, #C
Fort Worth, Texas 76137

817-338-1646
FAX: 817-338-4370

Charles W. Maxwell
1204 Fifth Avenue
Fort Worth, Texas 76014

817-336-7943
FAX: 817-336-2696

Eugene M. Kouri
2901 Lackland Road, #201
Fort Worth, Texas 76116

817-732-2821
FAX: 817-731-4273

R. Danford Doss
4200 Bryant Irvin Road, # 129
Fort Worth, Texas 76109

817-731-6964
FAX: 817-731-4273

Randall Barkley   817-732-3230
3600 Hulen Street, Suite B1   FAX: 817-732-4024
Fort Worth, Texas 76107-6868

While these listed specialize in pediatric dentistry, many others maintain a family dental practice and will often treat children as young as four or five years of age. My choice is:

Amy Bender, DDS   817-292-6090
4900 Overton Ridge
Fort Worth, Texas 76132

A call to the Dental Society will provide another list.

Chapter 20

Miscellaneous

Here comes a hodge-podge of information in no particular order. Are you looking for a caterer or a clown? A place to have a party or someone to bring one to your home? Flowers, cakes, or balloons? This is the place to start.

Planning a Party?

Several choices of places to find party supplies at reasonable prices in a variety of styles.

All About Parties
725-A Airport Freeway
Hurst, Texas 76053
817-268-1478

Party Package
5136 W. Vickery Blvd.
Fort Worth, Texas 76107
817-732-4088

This is a *rental* source for party supplies.

Party Warehouse
6659 McCart
817-370-0184

6550 Camp Bowie
817-737-7664

The Party Place
5316 Woodway Drive
Fort Worth, Texas
817-292-7396

Rent a tent, chairs, tables, or a punchbowl. Everything necessary for a backyard—or indoor—shindig.

They'll deliver it, too.

Balloons

Balloons Fantastique

Balloon greetings for any occasion. Or balloons for party decorations. Their spectacular arrangements can be delivered anywhere in the Metroplex. Want them shipped? They'll send balloons anywhere in the continental United States, Alaska, and Hawaii. Call 1-800-27-HAPPY (42779).

1607 W. Berry Street   817-923-9011
Fort Worth, Texas 76110   FAX: 817-924-8065
www.cowtown.net/users/balloon_hotline

Flowers

Too many florists to enumerate. Some that deliver and guarantee their products are:

Benbrook Floral   817-249-0112
406-D Mercedes Street   1-800-232-1673
Benbrook, Texas 76126

Gordon Boswell
1220 Pennsylvania Avenue   6200 Camp Bowie Blvd.
Fort Worth, Texas 76104   Fort Worth, Texas 76116
817-332-2265   817-738-9287

Lige Green
1300 8th Avenue   2111 Matlock Road
Fort Worth, Texas 76104   Arlington, Texas 76010
817-926-7171   817-277-8166
                                        Metro: 817-261-4162

Photography

Pictures keep the memories. Anyone can *take* a picture now that cameras come with film and flash built-in. Serious amateur photographers can even *make* a photograph, but it takes a *pro* to capture a special moment and turn it into art.

If you take your own—and most of us do most of the time—there's no place like Wolf Camera to supply film or single-use cameras. Their in-store lab processes any color print film, often in only an hour, and makes 4"x6" Wolfprints. Join the "Wolfpack" for a nominal annual fee and the second set of prints is free. Plus, get discounts on film, processing, and accessories. There are locations all around the Metroplex. Call 1-888-644-WOLF (9653) to find one near you. See their website (www.wolfcamera.com) for special offers and more information. Downloadable discount coupons are *always* on the site.

Jenny Solomon and Richard Heath, along with their knowledgeable sales people at the Camp Bowie Wolf's (817-731-2716), can suggest equipment and instruct on camera operation. They often repair minor problems while you wait. Ask about the magic machines enabling you to make enlargements from old prints, color slides, or negatives.

Wolf Camera also has a KIDS KORNER where junior photographers can get "Creature Cameras," Looney Tunes cameras and binoculars, "Taz" instant cameras, albums, and backpacks for their photo gear.

For processing of color slides and color print film, especially in medium or larger format (120 or 220), the choice is **The Slide Shoppe** (2525 W. 7th Street, Fort Worth, Texas 76107). Call Pat Denham or James Bradford (817-870- 1197) for answers to all questions photographic. The on-site lab allows for all manner of special services for the dedicated photographer. They are open Monday-Friday 8 A.M.-5 P.M.

Special occasions like weddings, proms, births, may call for a more experienced touch. For these events don't forget to plan well in advance, because the best professional photographers are often booked months ahead. Start saving for the wedding photography package when your daughter is born, 'cause it will COST! But nothing worth having is free. There are dozens of photographers in the Metroplex. Ask friends for their experiences and recommendations. Visit the studios and examine the work before deciding.

For some of the best work at a reasonable price, try:

Dalton Photography

Rick Dalton, a former Star-Telegram newspaper staff photographer, has turned his experienced eye toward more artistic visions. Visit his Benbrook studio to examine his superb wedding and family photographic endeavors.

8507 Highway 377 @ I-20   817-249-4918
Fort Worth, TX 76126   1-877-249-4918

Candles

Children shouldn't play with fire, but scented candles safely out of reach can add pleasure to the atmosphere. And the kids have to go to sleep *sometime*.

Dee Jay's Candles by Diane

Highest recommendations for the Plumeria, Frangipani, and Orange Spice in votive and larger sizes. All types and sizes of candles available along with remarkable accessories. A great place to shop for gifts after you've bought something for yourself!

4333 W. Vickery   817-737-2355
Fort Worth, Texas 76107

Candles and More

Ernest and Betty Frost stock the finest scented, artistic candles and holders to go along with them in a "little shop of odors" next to the Winn Dixie in Benbrook.

9465 Highway 377 S   817-249-8468
Benbrook, Texas 76126

Fresh Fruit and Vegetables, Plants, Too

Circle J Farmers Market

Fresh fruit in season and vegetables right off the farm add zest to meals. But, that's not all. The Circle J also carries bedding plants and hanging baskets to spruce up the back yard.

3525 Alta Mesa   817-292-2203
Fort Worth, Texas 76133
Hours: Everyday 8 A.M.-6 P.M.
Closed some holidays (like July 4ᵗʰ)

Cake or Cookies

Cake Boutique

Custom designed cakes for all occasions. See below under Caterers, too.

How to get there: Exit Brentwood Stair from Loop 820 North. Turn right at the light and *immediately* right again on McClellan (near the Williams Chicken place).

1721 McClellan Court   817-457-1561
Fort Worth, Texas 76112   1-888-212-9404
FAX: 817-457-1597

Harper's Bluebonnet Bakery

A Fort Worth standard since 1934, the cakes, cookies, and pastries are still grand even though the Harpers are no longer in command (see Sundance Deli in Chapter 20).

The chocolate fudge cake is a special delight, but you may need a dose of insulin after eating a couple of bites.

3905 Camp Bowie Boulevard   817-731-4233
Fort Worth, Texas 76107

Caterers

When it's party time and you want to take part in the fun instead of staying in the kitchen, the solution is to let someone else do the cooking. Every supermarket (Tom Thumb, Kroger, Albertson's, Minyard) has a deli department that will prepare trays for any size group. They'll even do the whole meal for Thanksgiving or Christmas. Turkey with all the fixin's; ham and all the sides; you name it, they can do it.

Some places do it better than others do. Jason's Deli makes the fattest sandwiches, on trays for groups from eight to eighty.

The best-kept secret in Fort Worth is the White Eagle Deli.

White Eagle Deli

Give them a couple of days' notice, and trays of sandwiches too heavy to carry will be ready to feed your hungry students *and* their parents. Veggies on another tray and cheeses on a third should keep the party going as long as necessary.

1560 N. Sylvania Ave.   817-838-3821
Fort Worth, Texas 76111

Cake Boutique

In addition to designing some of the best custom-made cakes in Fort Worth, this bakery also provides full service catering and city wide delivery for their associated floral business. They make cakes for weddings, birthdays, graduations, and showers. They will provide hors d'oeuvres, food trays, and personalized invitations for all occasions. The cake, by the way, is never left unfinished.

1721 McClellan Court   817-457-1561
Fort Worth, Texas 76112   1-888-212-9404
FAX: 817-457-1597

Party Places

Clubhouse for Kids Only

The absolute NEATEST place to have a party. So neat, in fact, that a *Fort Worth Child* subscriber survey voted it the Best Place for a child's party in 1998 and 1999. The Clubhouse provides supervised play zones, which include mountain ("wall") climbing, tree house, market, craft barn, hospital, and computer areas. Play activities are designed for children from one to twelve.

There are party rooms for birthday groups (prices start at $85) and include cake and lemonade and a Clubhouse T-shirt for the birthday child. Extras such as pizza and ice cream can be added. Set-up *and* clean-up is included in the price!

The Clubhouse is also available for after-hours rental for private parties or lock-ins. Karaoke is one of the features at the Fort Worth location.

A second location in Bedford (817-868-1800) offers similar amenities. A room dedicated to space exploration has been added there.

6650 Camp Bowie Blvd, Suite 110   817-763-0707
Fort Worth, Texas 76116   FAX: 817-483-2284
Hours: Tuesday-Thursday 10 A.M.-8 P.M.
Friday-Saturday 10 A.M.-9 P.M., Sunday noon-6 P.M.
Admission: Adults and infants free, Children 2-12 years $6.95
Toddlers 12-23 months $4.95

Pottery Pad

Here's a unique idea. Choose a piece of pottery, paint it to your heart's content, then let the nice people here clean up. A party place, too, for birthdays, holidays, or showers.

4818 Camp Bowie Boulevard   817-927-7823
Fort Worth, Texas 76107
Story Time: Tuesday and Thursday 3:45-5 P.M.
Saturday 10:30 A.M.-noon

Clowns * Magicians * Jugglers

Entertainment Crazy

Once you have the party place, whether it's at your home or at one of the party spots, it's time to send in the clowns. Clowns come singly or in pairs ($85/hour for one; $150/hour for two). Their shows include magic, juggling, face painting, and balloon animals. They limit the maximum size of the group to ensure that every child is happy.

Entertainment Crazy can also supply someone who does only face painting so each child can leave to audition for *CATS*. They also have moonwalks (bounce buildings) and, for a slightly older crowd, can bring in a DJ, with prizes, to MC hula-hoop or twist contests and play age-appropriate music. DJs—recommended for groups of fifty or more—cost $300 for four hours.

817-467-3333   FAX: 817-467-6464
E-mail: Clown582@AOL.COM

Alterations

When something needs fixing, taking in, or letting out, these are the people to see. There are many others around town, so check with friends in your neighborhood to find one close to home.

Coronado's

Anything that needs tailoring? Bring it here. Not only can they make it fit properly, the Coronados can build what you want from scratch. Bring a pattern, choose your material, and put them to work.

5658 Westcreek Drive, Suite 200   817-346-2286
Fort Worth, Texas 76133

Lydia Tailor Shop

Lydia and her able staff alter or repair almost any garment, and she is willing to stitch the prom dress of your daughter's dreams from your material.

9477 Highway 377 South   817-249-2624
Benbrook, Texas 76126

Local TV Stations

All the networks can be received with local reception—quality depends on how high the antenna goes—from east of Dallas to west of Fort Worth. Networks and their channels are as follows:

FOX	Channel 4
NBC	Channel 5
ABC	Channel 8
CBS	Channel 11
PBS	Channel 13
UPN	Channel 21
WB	Channel 33

Cable and Satellite are readily available all around the region.

What's on the Radio?

What do you like? Chances are you can hear it.

Kids:

AM:	620 KAAM(DISNEY)		1360 KAHZ

Country / C&W Music Stations:

FM:	93.1 KSTV	AM:	950 KDSX
	93.5 KIKT		1120 KCLE
	95.3 KHYI		1140 KJSA
	95.9 KYXS		1390 KBEC
	96.3 KSCS		1420 KPAR
	98.3 KBOC		1510 KSTV
	99.5 KPLX		
	105.3 KYNG		

Jazz/Classical/ Big Band:
FM: 88.1 KNTU
         88.7 KTCU
         89.1 KMQX
         89.5 KYQX
         92.1 KXEZ
         101.1 WRR
         107.5 KOAI

Oldies:
FM: 88.5 KEOM   AM: 1190 KLUV
         96.7 KMEO   1400 KGVL
         98.7 KLUV
         102.1 KTXQ

Rock/Contemporary:
FM: 92.5 KZPS   AM: 730 KKDA
         93.3 KKZN   910 KXEB
         94.5 KDGE
         97.1 KEGL
         97.5 KLAK
         97.9 KBFB
         100.3 KRBV
         102.9 KDMX
         103.7 KVIL
         104.5 KKDA
         105.7 KRNB
         106.1 KHKS

Sports/News/Talk:
FM: 90.1 KERA (NPR)   AM: 570 KLIF
                               820 WBAP
                              1080 KRLD
                              1220 KZEE
                              1310 KTCK
                              1700 KTCK

Religious:
FM: 88.3 KJCR   AM: 540 KDFT
         90.9 KCBI   660 KSKY
         91.7 KVTT   770 KPBC
         94.1 KLTY   970 KHVN
         94.9 KWRD   1040 KGGR

(Spanish) 1540 KTNO

Hispanic:

FM:		AM	
99.1 KHCK			870 KFJZ
106.7 KMRT			1270 KESS
106.9 KRVA			1440 KINF
107.1 KTLR			1480 KMRT
107.9 KICI			1540 KTNO
			1600 KRVA

Publications

Fort Worth Star-Telegram

The hometown paper founded by Amon Carter all those years ago has a circulation of around 250,000 (350,000 on Sunday) and readership of 675,700 daily (856,700 Sunday). It is available by home subscription and at newsstands and bookstores. One nice feature is free 2-line classified ads for items selling for less than $250. The Metro section of the paper is changed for different regions of the city/county so there is pertinent news for wherever you live or stay in addition to national, international, business, and sports reporting.

The Tuesday edition carries a weekly calendar of family events in the area.

The website provides current and back-issue content and links to lots of Fort Worth activities and attractions.

The Star-Telegram maintains a herd of Texas longhorns at its South Fort Worth printing facility. It is located off Hemphill Road south of Interstate 20. Drive by if you're in the neighborhood. These are *not* statues!

400 West Seventh Street
Fort Worth, Texas 76102

817-DEL-IVER (335-4837)
www.startelegram.com

Dallas Morning News

The *other* hometown paper. It is also available by subscription, at stores, and on the Internet at a superb website.

508 Young Street   214-977-7737
Dallas, Texas 75265-5237   www.dallasnews.com

Aledo Community News

This small newspaper from nearby Parker County gives coverage of local and regional events and is available as far away as Weatherford.

Fort Worth, Texas
The City's Magazine

A recent addition to the Fort Worth print media, this journal has been in publication since 1997. Devoted to Fort Worth residents' likes and dislikes, it features articles about food, recreation, homes, and current events. It also runs articles of historical interest and a photo section called "Worth Seeing," which shows what the "who's who" are doing. The back page is entitled "WorthLess"—you can guess what that's about.

3451 Boston Avenue   817-215-9125
Fort Worth, Texas 76116   www.magnoliamedia.com
Publisher: crisenhoover@mmgweb.com
Editor: wmcdonald@mmgweb.com

D Magazine

This, the *first* magazine of the Metroplex, has been around almost unchanged since 1967, except for a brief period of reorganization that angered a few readers and may have cost them some subscriptions. The magazine tends to concentrate on the Dallas end of the Meroplex, but coverage of the Mid-cities, Arlington, Grand Prairie, and Fort Worth isn't overlooked.

D does very good reviews of restaurants, theater, and musical entertainment along with frequent in-depth analyses of current politics and the local and regional economy. There are also occasional special editions such as the recent guide to dining. Check their wonderful website for the latest issue.

1700 Commerce Street, 18th Floor	214-939-3636
Dallas, Texas 75201-9636	Reprints: 1-800-256-8271
E-mail: feedback@dmagazine.com	www.dmagazine.com

Fort Worth Child

This free monthly newsmagazine is invaluable for parents (and grandparents, too) of younger kids—pre-school to pre-teen—who are curious about child development, parenting skills, health care, and educational and recreational activities. The July 1999 issue was "Simply the Best!"

Each edition has a calendar of what's going on in the community for kids and an excellent Party and Entertainment Guide in the back of the book.

4125 Keller Springs Road, Suite 146	972-447-9188
Addison, Texas 75001	FAX: 972-447-0633

Fort Worth Key Magazine

Through its distribution to area hotels and attractions as well as local chambers of commerce, *Key Magazine* gives a monthly report on activities, special events, tourism, and dining in the form of a digest-sized booklet that is easy to carry and simple to use. Individual subscriptions are available, but copies can often be obtained free of charge at any of the over 140 distribution points in Tarrant County.

The excellent website shows the current issue and selections from past editions. *Key* gives the most up-to-date information and carries advertising by many of the establishments and attractions that interest its readership.

3805 Ivywood court	817-654-9740
Arlington, Texas 76016	www.keymagfw.com
E-mail: keymagFW@aol.com	

Freebies

Several small newspapers are delivered locally to homes in the areas they serve and are available at restaurants and other public establishments such as City Hall. Their focus is on local community events and their support comes from advertisers doing business in the section of the city they cover.

Fort Worth Weekly

Fort Worth's alternative press, with an independent viewpoint, is geared to the 20- to 45-year-old crowd. It features articles about the "other" side of the news and does excellent reviews of restaurants, film, theater, and current club and musical performances. It is distributed free in bookstores and dining establishments.

1204-B W. Seventh Street
Fort Worth, Texas 76102
E-mail: words@fwweekly.com

817-335-WKLY (9559)
FAX: 817-335-9575
www.fwweekly.com

Benbrook Star

A new weekly paper for the Benbrook region. Managing Editor LynDee Stephens keeps the town folk informed and writes thoughtful editorials. Local businesses advertise specials.

119 Goliad Street, Suite 205
Benbrook, Texas 76126
E-mail: benbrookstar@thestargroup.com

817-249-7900
FAX: 817-249-7908
www.thestargroup.com

Benbrook Journal

Serving Benbrook, Western Hills, Ridglea West, Mont Del, Ridglea Country Club Estates, Meadows West, and western Fort Worth with local news and views. Issued every other Thursday and delivered to homes in the communities and shops and the establishments of its advertisers. Meme (Dorcas Neuman) keeps the whole town up-to-date on what's happening.

4305 Highway 377 S.   817-763-8574
Fort Worth, Texas 76116   FAX: 817-763-9105

Suburban Newspapers

For the residents of Benbrook, White Settlement, River Oaks, Sansom Park, Westworth Village, and the Joint Reserve Base. Charlesea D. Littlefield keeps a finger on the pulse. These come out on the Thursdays alternating with the Journal.

7820 Wyatt Drive   817-246-2473
Fort Worth, Texas 76108   FAX: 817-246-2474
Publishers of: *Benbrook News, White Settlement Bomber News, River Oaks News*

Shopping News

A trio of advertiser-supported community papers that notify the neighborhoods of local news and businesses. Carla Duke has the daily data.

Cityview * Ridglea * Wedgwood
6001 Granbury Road   817-292-2260
Fort Worth, Texas 76133

Rainy Day Activities

1.   **Read** to them. This can start with a trip to the public library. Reading to young children instills in them a love and appreciation for reading and teaches them to think in more than "sound bites."

2.   **Cook** with them. Bake cookies or a cake. Help them learn to follow directions and measure. Or combine both and get a copy of Mitchel Whitington's *Uncle Bubba's Chicken Wing Fling* (Republic of Texas Press, 1999). Read the tales of Cut Plug, Texas (a fictional town), and try the recipes (real recipes!) at the end of each chapter. Some are spicy; some are not. All are good. Doesn't everyone love chicken wings?

3.   When all else fails, there's Blockbuster! Everywhere.

Chapter 21

Calendar of Events, Month-by-Month

All events and attractions are subject to change. Be sure to call in advance to ascertain correct times, dates and locations.

January

New Year's Day • College football bowl games • Super Bowl

Will Rogers Center and Coliseum

For information call 817-871-8150 or 817-877-2400

- Southwestern Exposition and Livestock Show

Fort Worth Brahmas Professional Hockey

January-March at the Convention Center and the Will Rogers Memorial Center (see Chapter 7).

February

African-American History Month • Valentine's Day

Stockyards National Historic District: Cowtown Coliseum

- The Last Great Gunfight—Reenacted annually at the White Elephant Saloon. Call 817-624-9712 for information.

226

- Fort Worth Cowtown Marathon and 10K Run—A 10K, 5K, Marathon and 3-person Marathon Relay. Call 817-735-2033 for information.

Arlington Convention Center
For information, call 817-273-5222.
- Texas Rangers Mid-Winter Banquet and Carnival—Players honored. Call for more information.

March

St. Patrick's Day • March 17, Spring starts (Vernal Equinox)

Stockyards National Historic District
- Cowtown Goes Green—March 17, annually. For information call 817-626-7921.

Omni: Fort Worth Museum of Science and History
For information, call 817-732-1631.
- **Dolphins**: Swim with these amazing mammals and learn about their methods of communication in the splendor of the Imax film format. Call for prices and schedules.
- Ongoing: **Everest** and **The Great Migrations**.

Will Rogers Memorial Center
For information, call 817-221-2362.
- Fort Worth Kennel Club Dog Show

North Texas Irish Festival
Fair Park, Dallas. Call 214-670-8400 for information.

Metroplex Doll Club Show
Arlington Convention Center. Call 817-273-5222.

Annual Texas Storytelling Festival
Denton Civic Center Park Call 940-387-8336 for details. Or visit the Tejas Storytelling Association website: www.tejas-storytelling.com.

Spring Breakout at Six Flags
Call for information and dates: 817-640-8900, ext. 507.

April

Easter • Passover • Arbor Day/Earth Day • Daylight Savings Time begins

Will Rogers Equestrian Center
For information, call 817-871-8150.
- National Cutting Horse Association Super Stakes

Cowtown Coliseum
For information, call 817-625-1025.
- Easter at the Stockyards

Downtown Fort Worth
- Main Street Fort Worth Arts Festival—For Information call 817-336-ARTS (336-2787)
- Cinco de Mayo Celebration at Marine Park—The largest Hispanic event in North Texas. Call 817-834-4711 for details.

Irving Heritage Fair
At Irving Heritage Park, 2nd and Main Street. Call 972-259-1249 for dates and schedules.

Art Fiesta
Old Downtown Carrollton. Call 972-416-6600.

Scarborough Faire Renaissance Festival
Thirty minutes south of FW/D. Open Saturdays and Sundays (including Easter Sunday and Memorial Day Monday).

FM 66 Waxahachie, Texas   972-938-FAIR (938-3247)
www.scarboroughrenfest.com

Fort Worth Zoo
For information, call 817-871-7050, or look on the web at www.fortworthzoo.com.

- Zoo Run—A 5K Walk/Run plus a Kids Fun Run/Stroller Walk.

May

Mother's Day • Memorial Day

Mayfest

The annual celebration of spring along the banks of the Trinity River. Food, entertainment and educational displays for children of all ages. For information about Trinity Park, call 817-332-1055

Colonial Country Club

- MasterCard Colonial Invitational Golf Tournament—One of golf's major tournaments at Ben Hogan's home course. See trophy cases filled with Hogan memorabilia in the Clubhouse. Be prepared to struggle with parking!

Call for information: 817-927-4278.

Fort Worth Zoo

- Fort Worth Zoo Safari Open—A benefit for the Zoo with golf at a local course, catered lunch and dinner!

Downtown Fort Worth

For information, call 817-923-3121.

- A Little Night Run 5K—In the cool of the evening run a 5K starting and ending at the Worthington Hotel followed by a concert put on by the Youth Orchestra of Greater Fort Worth.

Bass Performance Hall

1-888-597-STAR(1-888-597-7827)

- Van Cliburn International Piano Competition
  May 25-June 11, 2001
  May 20-June 5, 2005
  May 22-June 7, 2009

Among the most prestigious piano competitions in the world since Van Cliburn returned triumphant from the 1959 Moscow Tchaikovsky Competition. Winners of *this* one can be assured of outstanding futures in the field of classical music performance. Contestants come to Fort Worth from all over the world and are hosted by local families. For information call 817-738-6536.

- Van Cliburn International Piano Competition for Talented Amateurs
  June 5-10, 2000
  Inaugurated in 1999, this was such a success, that it is being repeated in 2000, after which it will occur in alternate years.

Will Rogers Center and Coliseum

For information, call 817-871-8150.

- North Texas Arabian Horse Club
- Pro-Am Challenge Championships

June

Father's Day • First day of summer

Maverick Stadium

University of Texas at Arlington, Texas

- Annual Texas Scottish Highland Games—Find dates and hours on the web at www.texasscottishfestival.com.

Fort Worth Zoo

- Immunization Day—Free and low-cost immunizations at the Zoo provided by the Immunization Collaboration of Tarrant County. Children receiving shots get to take their families with them into the Zoo free for the day.

Fort Worth/Tarrant County Convention Center

For information, call 817-884-2222.

- Juneteenth Celebration—June 19th, of course. Unless it's on some other day. Call to verify.

Stockyards National Historic District: Cowtown Coliseum

- Quanah Parker Comanche Indian Pow Wow, Annual Chisholm Trail Roundup, and Tarrant County Fair
- Parade! Saturday. For information call 817-625-7005. Or find it on the web at www.chisholmtrail.org.

Texas Motor Speedway

NASCAR racing. Dates vary. Call 817-215-8520. Remember the Thursday Night Stampede (see Chapter 7).

Benbrook Summerfest

Call Chamber of Commerce.

July

Independence Day, July 4th

Fort Worth Zoo

New babies. Varies from year to year. Call 817-871-7050 to find out who's new at the Zoo.

Fort Worth/Tarrant County Convention Center

- Miss Texas Scholarship Pageant—For additional information, call 817-921-5577.

Banks of the Trinity

- Fourth of July Fireworks—Fireworks displays are done all "OVER" north Texas on or close to July 4th.

Will Rogers Equestrian Center

For information, call 817-871-8150.

- American Paint Horse Association World Championship Show
- National Cutting Horse Association Summer Cutting Spectacular

White Elephant Beer Garden
For information, call 817-626-2855.
* Railroad Day

Main Street
For information, call 817-343-8843.
* Fiesta Fort Worth—Another Hispanic festival. Call for date and time.

Botanic Garden
* Concerts in the Garden—Fort Worth Symphony Orchestra. Watch the newspaper or call 817-871-7686 for details. June and July.

August
Legends Car Racing at Texas Motor Speedway • National Night Out Against Crime: First Tuesday

Stockyards National Historic District: Cowtown Coliseum
* Pioneer Days

September
Fall begins (Autumnal Equinox) • Labor Day

Stockyards National Historic District: Cowtown Coliseum
* Pioneer Days
* Dash for the Timber—A 5K race to benefit the Amon Carter American Masters Collection. For information call 817-738-1933.
* Bike to Brazos—150-mile, two-day cycling tour from Fort Worth to Glen Rose and back. Benefites Multiple Sclerosis Society. Call 817-877-1222 ext. 61.

October
Halloween • Daylight Savings Time Ends

Will Rogers Equestrian Center

For information, call 817-871-8150.

- American Miniature Horse Association Championship Show
- International Andalusian Horse Assoc. Championship Show

Fort Worth/Tarrant County Convention Center

- Oktoberfest

Alliance Airport

For information, call 817-870-1515.

- Fort Worth International Air Show—Call for dates and directions.
- Halloween at Stockyards Station—October 31, annually. For information call 817-625-9715.

Fort Worth Zoo and Aquarium

- Boo at the Zoo—Dates to be announced. Check the papers, try the web site, or watch the big sign in front of the Zoo entrance on University. Kids trick-or-treat through the Zoo!

Scarborough Faire

- Screams at Scarborough Faire—Friday, Saturday, and Sunday nights in October

  Gates open at 7 P.M. Prepare to be scared!

  $15.99 per person includes parking and admission to all attractions, shows and special events. Children under six free. Group packages for 20 or more (call 972-938-3247 ext. 12).

November

Thanksgiving

Will Rogers Coliseum

For information, call 817-871-8150.

- Moslah Temple Shrine Circus—Tickets $6-$12. Prizes at each performance. During intermission, the kids can get rides on ponies and elephants.

Will Rogers Equestrian Center

For information, call 817-871-8150.

- Appaloosa Horse Club World Championship Show
- National Cutting Horse Association Championship Futurity

Downtown Fort Worth

- Parade of Lights—Sponsored by the *Fort Worth Star Telegram* and Downtown Fort Worth, Inc., this annual event includes lighted floats, antique cars, marching bands and choirs, lighting of the City Christmas Tree and a visit from Santa Claus. Clowns and equestrian units participate along with local beauty queens. For information call 817-336-2787.

- Jingle Bell Run—This one benefits the Arthritis Foundation. It is held each year on the Saturday following Thanksgiving in conjunction with the Parade of Lights and Christmas tree lighting ceremony and includes a 5K Night Run, 5K Fun Walk, and 1 Mile Elf Run. Registration fees ($20 on race day, less in advance) aid arthritis sufferers and entitle participants to jingle bells and T-shirts commemorating the event.

NorthPark Centre

For information, call 214-361-6345.

- The Trains at NorthPark—Vintage toy trains in a huge display reproducing many U.S. scenes, including the Dallas skyline and the Golden Gate Bridge. Proceeds benefit the Ronald McDonald House of Dallas. Discount tickets available at local Tom Thumb stores.

Fort Worth/Tarrant County Convention Center

- Holiday Pageant—Call 817-884-2222 for dates.

- Train Collectors Show—Call 817-884-2222 for dates.

December

Winter begins • Christmas, December 25

Downtown Fort Worth Festivities

- Heart of the Holidays
- Tuba Christmas General Worth Square
- Race for the Human Race—Call 817-877-1448 to confirm.

Will Rogers Equestrian Center

- National Cutting Horse Association Championship Futurity

Fort Worth Stockyards

- The T tour of Lights—Stockyards Station. Call 817-625-9715 for specifics.
- Stockyards Christmas Parade
- Christmas in the Stockyards—Activities throughout the month. Call 817-626-7921 to get details and schedules.

Fort Worth Zoo

- Zoobilee of Lights—Check the website (www.fortworth-zoo.com).

Chapter 22

Day Excursions to Surrounding Communities

While Fort Worth proper is loaded with activities and attractions sure to hold the interest of everyone in the family, there are, within a day's drive, scores of other places to see and things to do. For a more in-depth look at Dallas and San Antonio, the reader is referred to the titles in this series dealing with those cities (*Exploring Dallas with Children* and *Exploring San Antonio with Children*). If you have a long weekend, most of east Texas is accessible by automobile. To see the western half of the Lone Star State, however, you'll have to fly. It helps to remember that this place was once a country all its own. And Texarkana is closer to Chicago than it is to El Paso.

So, pack a picnic lunch, jump in the car, and set out to find adventure! In less than an hour you can travel back in time to the middle ages or visit a modern university, winery, or theme park.

Waco

In less than two hours, you can drive from the Trinity River Valley to that of the Brazos, one of the longest waterways in the state. The Waco Indians set up teepeekeeping in the late 1700s in what became a major city bearing their name. In

1870 a suspension bridge over the Brazos River at Waco provided the only crossing point for the followers of the Chisholm Trail. Built by the New York Firm of John A. Roebling Co., it became a model for the Brooklyn Bridge, also built by Roebling. But it's not for sale.

There are diversions and amusements to keep all ages enthralled during a visit to this vibrant municipality. Waco has parks (Cameron Park, Lion's Park), theaters (Hippodrome Theater, Waco Civic Theater), museums and libraries (Taylor Museum of Waco History, Lee Lockwood Library and Museum), shopping (Lake Air Mall, St. Basil's Market), fossils—not merely the kind who teach at the University—and a trolley.

Call the Waco Tourist Information Center (1-800-922-6386) for details about the Waco FunFare Ticket, which can get you discounts on many admission prices.

Start your tour with the:

Waco Convention and Visitors Bureau

Waco Convention Center   254-750-5810
100 Washington Avenue   Toll-free: 800-321-9226
P.O. Box 2570
Waco, Texas 76702-2570

Then choose from among some of these:

Baylor University

Chartered in 1845, Baylor is the oldest institution of higher education in the state of Texas and the largest Baptist University in the world. The University moved to Waco from Independence, Texas, in 1886. It is the first thing the visitor sees upon entering the city on I-35 from the north. (TCU also spent a few years in Waco, relocating to Fort Worth in 1910 after fire destroyed its main building.)

The campus is small enough for a pedestrian to cross in less than thirty minutes, but it supports 13,000 students in 158 bachelors degree programs, 23 masters, and 17 doctoral curricula, to say nothing of the Medical and Dental Schools at distant locations (Houston and Dallas, respectively).

The University is, itself, a tourist destination with several important attractions.

P.O. Box 97048   254-710-2407
Waco, Texas 76798   1-800-BAYLOR-U (229-5678)
www.baylor.edu

Armstrong Browning Library

Containing the world's largest collection of works by and reference materials relating to Robert Browning, the Armstrong Library is set in a magnificent structure with 56 stained glass windows portraying scenes from Browning poetry. It also has major works by his wife (Elizabeth Barrett Browning), Charles Dickens, Ralph Waldo Emerson, Matthew Arnold, and other 19th-century notables.

Dr. Andrew Joseph Armstrong taught at Baylor from 1912 until his death in 1954, inspiring generations of students and bringing to the campus numerous literary and dramatic masters. The library bearing his name honors his memory and promotes his vision.

Baylor Campus, 700 Speight   254-710-3566
Waco, Texas
Hours: Monday-Friday 9 A.M.-5 P.M., Saturday 9 A.M.-noon
Admission: Free

Strecker Museum

History, archeology, and paleontology all have a place in this basement display. Pleiosaur, elephant and giant turtle skeletons, Eskimo sled dogs, whale skull, Maori idols and pre-Colombian artifacts are but a few of the things exhibited here.

It is named in honor of John K. Strecker, who was director from 1903 to 1920. The museum, however, is the oldest continuously operating one in Texas, having come to Waco with Baylor in 1886.

Not yet open to the public, but affiliated with the Strecker Museum, is the Waco Mammoth Site (near the confluence of the Bosque and Brazos Rivers) where fossilized remains of fifteen of these animals were unearthed between 1978 and 1985. Limited tours can be arranged by advance reservation. Call the museum for information.

Sid Richardson Building 254-710-1110
Baylor Campus
Hours: Monday-Saturday 10 A.M.-4 P.M.
Closed Sundays and major holidays
Admission: Free

Ollie Mae Moen Discovery Center

In what was once a Waco grade school, this children's museum is actively involved as an outreach center with the school district. Participatory programs on natural history and science are by appointment. One day each February and October the public is invited for "Creatures and Culture." Call for details.

815 Columbus Avenue 254-757-0922
Waco, Texas
Hours: Monday-Friday 9 A.M.-4:30 P.M.
Closed Saturday and Sunday
Admission: Free (donations accepted) School groups $1/child.

Governor Bill and Vara Daniel Historic Village

An 1890s Texas village moved from Liberty County to its present spot on the banks of the Brazos gives visitors a taste of rural life from 100 years ago. On the thirteen-acre site are homes, school and church buildings, a saloon, blacksmith shop, livery stable, and cotton gin.

University Parks Drive off IH-35 254-710-1160

Waco, Texas
Hours: Tuesday-Friday 10 A.M.-4 P.M., Saturday-Sunday 1 P.M.-5 P.M.
Closed Mondays and holidays
Admission: Adults $3, Seniors $2, Students (K-college) $1
Baylor students, staff and faculty free.

Martin Museum of Art

Frequently changing exhibits of visual arts, including work by Baylor faculty.

Baylor Campus
Hooper-Schaefer Fine Arts Center
1401 S. University Parks Drive
Hours: Tuesday-Friday 10 A.M.-5 P.M., Saturday noon-5 P.M.
Also open during performances of Baylor Theater and other special events in the Hooper-Schaefer Fine Arts Center.
Admission: Free

Texas Ranger Hall of Fame

Located in Fort Fisher Park, this complex includes the Hall of Fame, the Homer Garrison Museum, and the Moody Texas Ranger Memorial Library. It showcases the lore and legend that led to the saying: "One riot, one Ranger." The star isn't all that makes the Ranger special. The Texas Rangers is the oldest state law enforcement agency in the country.

In the museum you will see items such as Jim Bowie's Bowie knife, Billy the Kid's Winchester carbine, and weapons used by Bonnie Parker and Clyde Barrow. Texas Ranger Frank Hamer, after tracking them for 102 days, captured them in Louisiana.

The library showcases books (what else!) as well as photographs and other historical material about the Rangers.

Got a computer whiz at home? Go to this Waco website: www.waco-texas.com/lev2.cfm/78 and print the page displayed. Take it to the Ranger Hall of Fame for an admission discount.

IH-35 at University Parks Drive   254-750-8631

www.wacocvb.com/txranger.htm
Hours: Daily 9 A.M.-5 P.M.
Closed Thanksgiving, Christmas Day, New Year's Day
Admission: Adults $4, Children $2, Group rate $3

Texas Sports Hall of Fame

The Tom Landry Theater and various interactive displays give children—adults, too—an opportunity to relish sports history. Really five museums in one, it contains the Texas Sports Hall of Fame, Texas Baseball Hall of Fame (with a life-size statue of Nolan...guess who), Texas Tennis Hall of Fame, and the Texas High School Halls of Fame for Football and Basketball.

1108 South University Parks Drive   254-756-1633
IH-35, Exit 335B   www.wacocvb.com/tshof.htm
Waco, Texas
Hours: Monday-Saturday 10 A.M.-5 P.M., Sunday noon-5 P.M.
Admission: Adults $4, Seniors and students $3.50
Group rate $2

Cameron Park Zoo

In 416-acre Cameron Park one of central Texas' finest small zoos displays its animal collection in enclosures replicating as closely as possible their natural habitat. A new herpetarium shows off an excellent reptile collection.

The park also has mountain bike trails, a disc golf course (that's golf with Frisbees—sounds interesting, doesn't it?) and Miss Nellie's Pretty Place, a lovely garden that can be rented for parties or weddings and is a favorite spot for photography.

1701 North Fourth Street   254-750-8400
Waco, Texas   FAX: 254-750-8430
www.waco-texas.com/zoo/
Hours: Monday-Saturday 9 A.M.-5 P.M., Sunday 11 A.M.-5 P.M.
Closed Thanksgiving, Christmas and New Year's Day
Admission: Adults $4, Children 4-12 $2 (under 3 free)
Seniors 60 and older $3.50

Discounts for groups of 20 or more.

Dr. Pepper Museum

In 1885, when pharmacist Charles Curtis Alderton, working at the Old Corner Drug Store, and beverage chemist R. S. Lazenby combined the flavors for the drink that became Dr Pepper, the world was still a year away from Coca Cola. Originally called the "Waco" because it could be obtained nowhere else, the formula was so successful that it remains unchanged to the present day. The original bottling plant, now listed on the National Register of Historic Places, is the home of the Dr Pepper Museum.

Visitors to the museum are shown the history of the soft drink industry. They view manufacturing and bottling equipment, interactive displays, and a TV showing old Dr Pepper commercials, including Barry Manilow's "Wouldn't you like to be a Pepper, too?"

In the gift shop you can deck the entire family out as Peppers!

300 South Fifth Street   254-757-1024
Waco, Texas   www.drpeppermuseum.com
Hours: Monday-Saturday 10 A.M.-4 P.M., Sunday noon-4 P.M.
Admission: Adults $4, Seniors $3.50, Students $2
Groups $.50/ticket discount

Brazos Trolley

Summertime visitors to Waco may want to leave their cars and ride in the air-conditioned comfort of the Trolley to see the main attractions (Texas Ranger and Dr Pepper Museums, Suspension Bridge, Cameron Park Zoo, Convention Center, Sports Hall of Fame and others). Departures are every 20 minutes on Saturday and every 35-45 minutes daily and Sunday from the Tourist Information Center. From September-November and March-May it runs only on weekends.

Fare: Adults $.50, Seniors and students $.25
Children under 5 FREE with an adult (Exact change required.)

Waxahachie

The seat of Ellis County has served as the setting for several well-known motion pictures (*Places in the Heart* springs first to mind) and once played a role as a stop along the Chisholm Trail. Far enough away from Dallas to maintain its own identity, it is close enough to count—almost—as a suburb.

The restored Chautauqua Auditorium in Getzendaner Park is one of many structures in Waxahachie now on the National Register of Historic Places.

Scarborough Faire

Join the Society for Creative Anachronism and return to Merrie Olde England in the time of Henry the Eighth. Or go only to observe; the enjoyment is much the same. No one, however, can resist the excitement. Located on 35 wooded acres near Waxahachie, Scarborough Faire® is *the* Renaissance Festival. Ten stages distributed about the grounds offer continuous entertainment. More than 200 craftspeople and artisans demonstrate occupations such as glassblowing, printing (on the Gutenberg Press), blacksmithing, and flutemaking. Their products are available for purchase in shops throughout the Faire.

Twice a day the King and his Queen—Anne Boleyn (unless she loses her head!)—emerge to observe the Royal Joust along with the assembled spectators. Numerous other performances prevent boredom from burgeoning. Moreover, rides and games of skill and chance give the guests an opportunity to share the medieval mindset. Some include: Drench a Wench, Fight the Knight, Elephant and Camel Rides, Darts and Crossbows. Turtle races, face painting, and a petting zoo bestow a "spot of fun" upon younger members of the company.

If Mom or Dad is a serious amateur photographer, there is an annual Scarborough Faire photography contest with a chance to win season passes for the following year, limited edition T-shirts, and beer steins.

Then, there's the food! The trademark giant turkey leg is only one of more than 60 edibles available at stalls all around the acreage. Bring your appetite!

South of the Metroplex   972-938-FAIR (938-3247)
Off IH-35E at Exit 399A   www.scarboroughrenfest.com
Waxahachie, Texas
Hours: 10 A.M.-7 P.M.
Saturdays and Sundays plus Memorial Day from Mid-April to the first weekend in June
Admission: Adult $15.99, Children 5-12 $6
Season passes available. Discount tickets at area Kroger Stores.
Parking included in admission price.

Victorian Homes

When you tire of 17th century Europe, take a drive through the city and view the many beautiful Victorian, Gothic Revival, and Queen Anne style homes. The gingerbread you'll see will be plentiful but inedible. More than half the Texas buildings listed on the National Register are located in Waxahachie.

Each June, Waxahachie stages the Gingerbread Trail, a Tour of Homes and other historically significant buildings. The festival also incorporates an Arts and Crafts Fair at the Chautauqua Campgrounds, an array of antique automobiles, and the opportunity to visit the specialty shops.

Call the Chamber of Commerce (972-938-9617 or toll-free 1-888-428-7245) for information, ticket discounts, and to place orders. Visa/MasterCard accepted.

The C-of-C website can assist: www.waxacofc.com.

In November look for the Candlelight Home Tour and Bethlehem Revisited, a Christmas Pageant. Check with the Chamber about this, too.

Ellis County Courthouse

This elaborate, ornate building dates from 1895 when Italian artisans were brought here to carve the exterior red sandstone and granite. At $150,000, it was quite high-priced for those days. The recurring face seen on the façade is said to represent Mabel Frame, the railroad telegrapher with whom one of the Italian sculptors became infatuated.

Ellis County Museum

Another restored 19th century building houses historic artifacts, photos, toys, and household furnishings typical of the early days of this region.

Courthouse Square
Hours: Tuesday-Saturday 9 A.M.-5 P.M.

Chautauqua Auditorium

The last remnant of a practice dating to the turn of the last century. Known as the Traveling Chautauquans, originally from upstate New York, this brought ministers, scientists, educators, statesmen, and entertainers to isolated parts of the country. The Auditorium, an octagonal structure, was built in 1902 and became the focal point of a tent city for two weeks every July until 1930. Celebrities such as William Jennings Bryan, Will Rogers, and the Marine Band appeared on its stage. It was restored in 1976 and is on the National Register. It still serves as a city auditorium and hosts the Fort Worth Symphony Orchestra several times a year.

Getzendamer Park
Waxahachie, Texas

Weatherford

West of Fort Worth lies Parker County with a population of more than 80,000 people. Founded in 1855, it was named for Isaac Parker, a pioneer legislator and the uncle of Cynthia

Ann Parker. She was taken as a child from her home during the Texas Revolution and raised by the Comanches, eventually marrying Peta Nacona. Their son Quanah Parker was the last of the great Comanche chiefs. Sometime, if you're headed into the Texas Panhandle, you may pass through tiny Quanah, the town named for him.

Any day of the week is a good one to visit Parker County Seat, Weatherford, but some may be more fruitful than others. The place to start a tour is at the:

The Weatherford Chamber of Commerce

The Chamber is housed in the old Santa Fe Railroad Depot. It still has many of the old copper and brass light fixtures from the early days of train travel. In front of the Chamber building is a life-size bronze sculpture, the work of local artist Kelly Graham, depicting a cutting horse separating a calf from the (not shown) herd.

Be sure to ask about the mysterious Lake Monster (Man-Eating-Devil-Cow) of Weatherford.

401 Fort Worth Street   817-596-3801
P.O. Box 310   888-594-3801
Weatherford, TX 76086   www.weatherford-chamber.com
Hours: Daily 8:30 A.M.-5 P.M.

Go to Weatherford early any month for:

First Monday Trade Days

On the Friday, Saturday, and Sunday before the first Monday of each month people gather with things to sell at the Trade Grounds located at the intersection of Fort Worth Highway and Santa Fe Drive. For information call 817-598-4351. Remember: "One man's junk is another man's treasure."

First Monday is a Southwest regional tradition dating to the days when farmers would gather on the Courthouse Square to sell their produce and swap stories and news. It began in the 1850s when the circuit judge would arrive to hold court on the first Monday of the month.

What once took place on the first Monday, now occurs on the weekend preceding it, and Monday is business as usual.

While the one held in Weatherford is excellent, there's another First Monday in **Canton**, Texas (east of Dallas), that is spectacular. In Canton, First Monday may require two days to *see* everything.

In either place, bargains are to be had and good eats may be just around the next bend in the path. If you have "stuff" to sell, call 817-598-4351 for information about Weatherford Trade Days space rental. Find out more at the website: www.firstmonday.com.

Old Time Cowboy Gathering

Continuous free western entertainment provides a good time for all comers. There are poets, singers, and storytellers. See gunfight reenactments and buy western arts and crafts. Then go to the chuckwagon cook-off.

Peter Pan

What does the boy who wouldn't grow up have to do with Weatherford? Anyone who has lived near here for even a short time knows the answer. This was the home of Mary Martin, the Broadway star who created the role of Peter Pan. She and her late husband, Richard Halliday, are buried at City Greenwood Cemetery (visit to find graves of other famed local legends). The Heritage Public Library, 1214 Charles Street, has a fine exhibit of Martin memorabilia and a statue of puckish Peter Pan (sorry, no Tink!), sculpted by Ronald Thomason.

Chandor Gardens

Douglas Chandor, a British-born portraitist, came to Weatherford in 1934. He and his Weatherford native wife, Ina

Kuteman Hill Chandor, transformed a rocky hilltop property on Simmons Street into a wonderland garden. After his death in 1953, Mrs. Chandor maintained it until 1978 as a memorial to him. After her death, the garden deteriorated. Chuck and Melody Bradford began its restoration in 1994. It is once again open for tours. Call 800-826-1113 or the Chamber of Commerce (817-596-3801) for information.

Frontier Days Celebration Livestock Show and Rodeo

Sponsored by the Parker County Sheriff's Posse

An annual event in cutting horse country that has something for everyone. Call 888-594-3801 for more information.

Peach Festival

Over 200 arts and crafts sellers line Courthouse Square and York Avenue. Most years there are also *Peaches*! (Some past years have been marred by drought, leaving the trees barren.) And when the peaches are there, you'll have peach cobbler, peach ice cream, fresh peaches, peach drinks. You'll even go home with Peach Festival T-shirts.

Three stages provide entertainment throughout the day. There will be an art show and craft competitions as well as children's amusement areas. The hardy can join the Peach Pedal bike riders (11 miles to 100K!).

9 A.M.-5 P.M.
Admission: Adults $3, Children 5 and up $1

Civil War Weekend

The third annual reenactment of actual engagements between Union and Confederate troops. Visitors get the opportunity to tour the camps and see how the soldiers and civilians lived (and died?).

For information, call 817-596-3801, 888-594-3801, or go to the website: http://weatherford-chamber.com/civil.htm.

Other things to do in Weatherford

- See the magnificent, three-story 1886 limestone Courthouse with its central clock tower.
- **Theater off the Square**, 319 York Avenue. Call 817-341-8687 for schedule and ticket information.
- **Candlelight Tour of Homes** Sponsored by the Parker County Heritage Society. Call 888-594-3801 for information.
- **National Champion Pecan Tree**, thought to be 1,000 years old, and the largest in the United States. Privately owned at 2712 North Main (Highway 51 North).
- **Pythian Home**: A replica of a European castle. Built in 1909 by the Knights of Pythias and in continuous use since as a refuge for homeless children. Tours by appointment.
- **J.Brown Stagecoach Works:** Making real stagecoaches and buggies for the movies. Tours by appointment, $3.00/person.
- **Holland Lake Park:** Log cabins with real bullet holes from Indian raids.
- **Farmers Market:** Fresh vegetables and those Parker County peaches, in season.

Denton

Only 36 miles north of Fort Worth, this town of 72,000 is the County Seat of Denton County. Founded in 1857 and named for soldier-lawyer-preacher John B. Denton, Denton combines small-town ambiance with metropolitan flair. Its historical, artistic, and cultural diversions make it another good locale in which to live or look around.

Nearby Exposition Mills provides discount shopping for all (see Chapter 13), and the picturesque downtown has more quaint shops and interesting restaurants. With two major university campuses, theater and music are easy to find.

On the way to Denton along IH-35W you will pass Alliance Airport (Airshow—see Chapter 4) and Texas Motor Speedway (see Chapter 7).

Contact the Chamber of Commerce for calendars and detailed information about all that Denton has to offer:

Denton Chamber of Commerce

414 Parkway
Denton, Texas 76201
940-382-9693
www.denton-chamber.org
E-mail: dcoc@global.net

P. O. Drawer P
Denton, Texas 76202
FAX: 940-382-0040
Toll free 888-381-1818

At town center start with:

Denton County Courthouse

A massive limestone construct like so many others in central Texas (see Waxahachie and Weatherford), it was designed in 1895 and restored in 1987. It has the characteristic central clock tower and the grave of John B. Denton on the grounds.

110 West Hickory
Denton, Texas

The building is home to:

Denton County Courthouse-on-the-Square Museum

The collection includes pottery, dolls and toys, Victorian handbags, Early American Pattern Glass, and an amusing Pecan Art exhibit of caricatures carved from the state nut.

110 West Hickory Street
Denton, Texas
www.co.denton.texas.us/dept/hcm.htm
Hours: Monday-Friday 10 A.M.-4:30 P.M., Saturday 11 A.M.-3 P.M.

940-565-5667

Evers Hardware

Still run by the founding family, this 100-year-old hardware store maintains many of the same fixtures and displays that it had when it first opened.

109 West Hickory   940-382-5513
Denton, Texas
Hours: Monday-Saturday 8 A.M.-5 P.M.

Hangar 10 Flying Museum

Four planes: Lockheed 10A (once owned by actress Margaret O'Brien), Beechcraft Stagger Wing, PT-22 Army Air Corps trainer, and a World War II reconnaissance Piper L-4.

Denton Municipal Airport   940-565-1945
1945 Matt Wright Lane
Denton, Texas
Hours: Monday-Saturday 8 A.M.-2 P.M.
Admission: Free

Daughters of the American Revolution Museum

The only collection of its kind in existence, it holds a succession of actual garments or faithful replicas of inaugural gowns worn by the wives of the governors of the state and presidents of the Republic of Texas. Created in 1940, the exhibit is regularly updated and now also has gowns of the wives of two U.S presidents (can you guess which ones?*).

Gowns of the First Ladies of Texas   940-898-3201
Texas Women's University
Human Development Building, first floor
117 Bell Avenue
Denton, Texas
Hours: Monday-Friday 8 A.M.-5 P.M.
Admission: Free

* Eisenhower and LBJ

Two other exhibits at TWU:

Women's Airforce Service Pilots (W.A.S.P.) Collection

and

Texas Women: A Celebration of History

TWU Campus   940-898-2665
Blagg-Huey Library   www.twu.edu

Other things to see and do in Denton

- Visit the websites of Texas Women's University (www.twu.edu) and the University of North Texas (www.unt.edu) to learn what's going on at their campuses.
- **Little Chapel in the Woods**: On TWU campus. Designed by O'Neil Ford and built in 1939. Ten stained glass windows by TWU art students depict "Woman Ministering to Human Needs." It is open during school hours and available for rental as a striking setting for weddings.
- **Pioneer Woman Statue**: On TWU campus.
- **Silk Stocking Row**: Victorian homes in the Oak-Hickory Historic District.
- **UNT Planetarium**: In the Environmental Education, Science and Technology building, corner of Hickory and Avenue C. Hours: Friday-Saturday 8 P.M. and Saturday-Sunday 2 P.M. A 110-seat planetarium, exhibit hall, outdoor learning area, and Native Texas Landscape. Call 940-565-3599 for information.
- **Rare Book Room and Texana Collections**: UNT Willis Library, room 437. Hours: Monday-Friday 9 A.M.-6 P.M. Permanent resource collection as well as major exhibits throughout the year. Call 940-565-2769 for information.
Website: www.library.unt.edu/dept.rarebook.

- **Texas Fashion Collection: UNT Scoular Hall**. Tours available for school groups. Call 940-565-2732 or write for information: UNT, Texas Fashion Collection, School of Visual Arts, Box 5098, Denton, Texas 76203-0098.
- **Texas Story Telling Festival**: April.
- **Christmas in Downtown:** Holiday Lights and Victorian Christmas at the Courthouse-on-the-Square each December.
- **Pilot Knob**: About four mile south of town on Highway 377, drive past a 900-foot hill said to have once been the hideout of notorious Texas outlaw Sam Bass, who was killed in Round Rock (near Austin).
- **Ray Roberts Lake State Park**: Two sections, Johnson Branch (940-637-2294) and Isle du Bois Unit (940-686-2148). Camping, boating, fishing, swimming, picnicking, and nice trails are found at both. Call 512-389-8900 for information about Texas State Parks. Website: www.tpwd.state.tx.us.

Granbury

Settled in 1854 and named for Confederate States General Hiram Bronson Granbury, this quaint town is 35 miles southwest of Fort Worth. As with many Texas towns, this one's center is dominated by the limestone Courthouse with its central clock tower. The Victorian Courthouse Square was added to the National Register of Historic Places in 1974, the first in Texas to make it.

The county seat of Hood County lays claim to some interesting legends and a few factual bits of historic lore. It is said that Jesse James spent his final years there and, rumor has it, so did John Wilkes Booth. He supposedly tended bar under the name John St. Helen.

Elizabeth Crockett, Davy's widow, definitely lived in Granbury. She and her children (Elvira Crockett Halford and Robert Patton Crockett) are buried in nearby Acton Cemetery. Their gravesite, Acton State Historical Park, is the smallest state park in Texas.

For more information contact the:

Granbury Convention and Visitors Bureau

100 North Crockett Street   817-573-5548
Granbury, Texas 76048   800-950-2212
www.granbury.org

From there cross the square to:

Hood County Jail

Start a circuit of the Square at the Visitors Center in the 1885 jail. The original cells and hanging tower remain to be inspected.

208 North Crockett Street
Tours: Monday-Friday 9 A.M.-5 P.M.
Saturday 10 A.M.-4 P.M., Sunday 1-4 P.M.

Granbury Opera House

The Opera House dates from 1886 but was unused for sixty years before its 1975 restoration. Now it is the home of a full-time production company doing live theater *every month*.

P. O. Box 297   817-573-9191
Granbury, Texas 76048   Metro 817-572-0881
www.granburyoperahouse.org

Billy Sol Estes Museum

Once considered one of America's oustanding young men, Billie Sol was a "Good Ol' Boy" gone bad. Meet Billie's daughter, Pamela, and browse through the memorabilia and antiques.

503 East Pearl Street
Granbury

Granbury Queen

A 73-foot replica of a Mississippi River paddle wheeler cruises Lake Granbury Saturday and Sunday afternoons between March and October. Departure is at 2 P.M. from river landing one mile south of Highway 377 on Texas 144. Call 817-573-6822 for information.

Elan Cruises

Another service touring the Brazos River. Small groups ride in open-air pontoon barges (charter service can be arranged for larger groups). Fares are from $15 to $30 per person. Call 1-800-841-5309 for more details about breakfast, dinner, and Murder-Mystery cruises.

Brazos Drive-In

Don't forget the drive-in movies (see Chapter 15).

General Hiram Granbury Civil War Reenactment

Held each year in September or October.

Cheyne Farm
FM 51

Great Race Automotive Hall of Fame

Great American Auto Library, twelve Great American race vehicles, videos, games, snacks, and memorabilia of the annual Boston-to-Sacramento vintage auto race.

114 North Crockett Street   817-573-5200
www.greatrace.com
Hours: Friday-Saturday 10 A.M.-6 P.M., Sunday noon-5 P.M.
Admission: $1

Fourth of July Parade

The parade is held annually on the Fourth of July on Granbury Courthouse Square. A Cowboy Fourth celebration.

Glen Rose

Comanche Peak Nuclear Power Station

Program, exhibits, tour of nuclear power plant. Call for information.

Visitor Information Center   254-897-5554
Highway 56 North
Glen Rose, Texas
Monday-Saturday 9 A.M.-4 P.M.
Admission: Free

The Promise

Since its premiere in 1989 this open-air production has gained strength and reputation. With a cast of more than 100 actors, singers, and dancers, it portrays the story of the life of Christ. Ticket prices range from $8-$19.

Other concerts are held in the amphitheater throughout the remainder of the year. Call 817-897-4509 for more information.

Texas Amphitheater   254-897-4341
P. O. Box 927   254-897-3932
Glen Rose, Texas 76043   800-687-2661
E-mail: promise@itexas.org   FAX: 254-897-3388
Fridays and Saturdays June-October 8:30 P.M.

Fossil Rim Wildlife Refuge

Visit deepest Africa without the need for a passport (see Chapter 6).

P. O. Box 2189   254-897-2960
Glen Rose, Texas 76043   www.fossilrim.com

Dinosaur Valley State Park

This scenic park holds 1,500-acres straddling the Paluxy River slightly northwest of Glen Rose. Opened in 1972, the region was once (113 million years ago) the shore of an Inland Sea. The river has cut away the softer sediment and exposed preserved dinosaur tracks in its bed.

Fiberglass models of a 70-foot Apatosaurus and a 45-foot Tyrannosaurus Rex, built for the Sinclair Oil Company's exhibit at the 1964 New York World's Fair, have been donated to stand guard at the Park.

Other park activities are available (camping, biking, picnicking, horseback riding, hiking). Part of the state longhorn herd can be found there, too. Wildlife is plentiful.

P. O. Box 396   254-897-4588
Glen Rose, Texas 76043   800-792-1112
www.tpwd.state.tx.us/park/dinosaur/dinosaur.htm
Hours: Daily 8 A.M.-10 P.M.

Dallas

Thirty miles to the east, the lesser half of the Metroplex still has much to offer. Replete with museums, theatrical entertainment, excellent dining, and a fine zoo, the faster-paced life of our sister city is best enjoyed in small doses.

However, when you are ready to do it there are several things to remember. First, never forget that Big D is BIG. And everyone is always driving, especially on Central Expressway (the world's second longest parking lot), a road that is *forever* under construction.

In the past thirty years, the population of Dallas has grown—as has that of Fort Worth (Cowtown is projected to reach 500,000 by 2002)—and most of them are Yankees. But we should be tolerant; after all, they *want* to be here.

Most important, when you plan to visit Dallas take a guide. If you can't find a native, get a copy of Kay McCasland Threadgill's *Exploring Dallas with Children* (Republic of Texas Press, second edition, 1998).

San Antonio

The Alamo City is only six or seven hours by car from Fort Worth. Although it is possible to go there for a long weekend, it is impossible to see it all in such a short time. A better idea is to *move* there and take a few years to soak it all up.

Riverwalk, Fiesta Texas, Sea World, The Alamo each deserve, no, *require*, a full day or more. One site not to be missed is the Alamo Museum maintained by the Daughters of the Texas Republic. To really enjoy San Antonio, as with Dallas, a guide is a good thing. Your guide in San Antonio is Docia Schultz Williams (*Exploring San Antonio with Children*, Republic of Texas Press, 1998).

Chapter 23

Lodging

Hotels

There are dozens of hotels in Fort Worth and more in Arlington and the mid-cities. Dallas is well stocked, too. New motels keep popping up all around the town. While there isn't space to deal with all, a few words will be devoted to the more noteworthy. The *most* noteworthy would be:

The Worthington Hotel

This is Fort Worth's only four-star, four-diamond hotel. Take a week or a weekend and get pampered. With the Star of Texas Grill and Reflections Restaurant (also earning four diamonds) in addition to the Sunday Brunch and a sufficiency of surrounding dining destinations, no one need go hungry. Also within walking distance there are bookstores, gift and clothing shops, movie theaters, and Bass Performance Hall.

The Tarrant County Courthouse—as seen on *Walker, Texas Ranger,*—is also a short walk from the Worthington. In front of the northeast corner of the Courthouse is a fountain for watering horses, a recent renovation of one that had been there from 1892 until it fell into disrepair in the early 1940s. The reconstruction was part of the Fort Worth Sesquicentennial efforts to remember the days when cowboys sat tall in the saddle, rather than in pickup trucks and Suburbans.

Although a bit pricey for our town the $200-225 average room rate would scarcely fluster a New Yorker. Since they sometimes run a "weekend getaway" special, the Worthington experience is often affordable to all.

200 Main Street   817-870-1000
Fort Worth, Texas   800-433-5677
FAX: 817-335-3847

The striking edifice—now known as the Renaissance Worthington—is at the western extreme of downtown. At the other end is:

The Radisson Plaza Fort Worth

The Radisson Plaza gained fame in 1963, when it was the Hotel Texas. President John Fitzgerald Kennedy spent his last night in room 805 and gave what turned out to be his last speech in front of the hotel before leaving for the motorcade in Dallas where he lost his life.

With an average room rate of $155, this three-diamond facility offers a spacious lobby with gift shops, comfortable lounging and dining accommodations. It is a short block from the Tarrant County Convention Center and thus a favorite for visitors attending functions there.

815 Main Street   817-870-2100
Fort Worth, Texas   800-333-3333
FAX: 817-335-3408

Almost midway between these two is:

Blackstone Courtyard by Marriott

The 23-story, 268-foot-tall building from the 1920s is Fort Worth's only "New York" style skyscraper, featuring multiple setbacks leading to its spired top. It has recently been restored and returned to productive use by the Marriott Corporation.

Marriott operates several Courtyard hotels in Fort Worth as well as Residence Inns with kitchen-equipped suites at reasonable rates. There is a Courtyard almost directly across University Avenue from a Residence Inn, both within walking distance of the Zoo.

601 Main Street   817-885-8700
Fort Worth, Texas 76102   FAX: 817-885-8303

Etta's Place

This little B & B (Bed and Breakfast) evokes memories of the wild old days of Hell's Half Acre. The name comes from Etta Place, Butch Cassidy's "lady" friend. It has ten bedrooms in central Fort Worth close to all downtown amusements.

200 West Third Street   817-654-0267
Fort Worth, Texas 76102   FAX: 817-878-2560

Stockyard Hotel

109 East Exchange Avenue   817-625-6427
Fort Worth, Texas   800-423-8471
FAX: 817-624-2571

and

Miss Molly's Hotel

Both of these will set you right in the heart of the Northside Stockyards area. Walk to Billy Bob's Texas, the Stockyards museum, shops, and restaurants. A few blocks more will take you to Stockyards Station to board the Tarantula Train for a run to Grapevine.

Miss Molly's has a "slightly risque" air—once upon a time, they say, it *may* have been a brothel. Now it behaves and *is* a stylish B & B with rooms decorated in period style much as they were when it was new in 1910. The parlor has antique furniture beneath a stained glass skylight where guests find breakfast or a quiet place to read a paper or chat with new friends. Rooms are named for "Cowboys," "Oilmen," "Cattlemen," "Gunslinger." There are also rooms for the girls, including "Miss Josie's," the madam (the only room with a private bath).

Miss Molly's is a place for older children and grownups. Discounts are offered on Sunday through Thursday and larger discounts to riders of the Tarantula Train.

109 ½ West Exchange Avenue   817-626-1522
Fort Worth, Texas 76106   800-99-MOLLY (996-6559)
FAX: 817-625-2723

Motels

All the major chains have representation in Fort Worth. A recent surge in building has brought new lodging to the southwest part of the city with La Quinta, AmeriSuites, Studio Plus, Holiday Inn Express, Extended Stay America and Towne Place Suites by Marriott. Hampton Inn, on the south side of IH-20 east of Bryant Irvin Road puts you within walking distance of Hulen Mall (see Chapter 13).

Dude Ranches

Most of the dude ranches in the Metroplex are for parties and other single day functions. They do not have facilities for overnight stays. If you are interested in a real "ranching" vacation, try the Flying L in Bandera (see below).

Canyon Lake Ranch

Ten miles south of Denton, one mile west of IH-35 from Exit 458. Prefer corporate meetings, convention parties, or company picnics. Facilities include swimming, fishing, games, hay rides, trail rides, and cook outs.

P.O. Box 206   940-321-2840
Lake Dallas, Texas   FAX: 940-321-3415

Texas Lil's Diamond A Ranch

Texas Lil's has been catering to those with a Western hankering for over 20 years. The place can handle groups from 20 to 2,000, but even solo guests will be made welcome.

They are equipped to handle weddings and wedding receptions, theme parties, church, school, and club activities, and family reunions. Birthday parties should be a snap.

Come early for a "Cowboy Breakfast" or stay for a "City Slicker Cattle Drive." Call for reservations and pricing (price per person depends on the size of the group).

P.O. Box 665   940-430-0192
Justin, Texas 76247   800-LIL-VILL (545-8455)
E-mail: texaslil@texaslils.com   www.texaslils.com

Other area dude ranch choices:

Circle R Ranch

5910 Cross Timbers Road   940-430-1561
Flower Mound, Texas 75028

Double Tree Ranch

310 Highland Village Road   972-317-5000
Lewisville, Texas 75067

Flying L Guest Ranch

A Texas Hill Country Resort vacation spot for the whole family or for loosening up stodgy corporate types.

Horseback and hay rides, golf course and driving range, swimming pool, tennis courts, playground, and petting corral should give every member of the group something to please them. There's even a General Store.

P.O. Box 1959   830-460-3001
Bandera, Texas 78003   800-292-5134
www.flyingl.com   FAX: 830-796-8455

Campgrounds and State Parks

State parks in both Oklahoma and Texas are within easy reach of Fort Worth and Dallas for day trips or overnight stays. Most of the parks have camping facilities as well as swimming, fishing, boating, and trails for hiking, biking, and sometimes horseback riding. Texas Parks and Wildlife Department will provide details. Decide where you want to go, get a map, and log on to www.tpwd.state.tx.us. Everything you need to know can be found on that site.

Going to Oklahoma? To find out about one of our northern neighbor's 50 state parks call or write:

Oklahoma Tourism and Recreation Department

Ask for the Oklahoma Vacation Guide. Two useful websites are:
www.touroklahoma.com and www.traveloklahoma.com.

15 North Robinson, Suite 100   405-521-2471
Oklahoma City, OK 73102   FAX: 405-232-2562

Bed and Breakfast

These are generally small, with limited numbers of rooms, and work best for small families with infants or more mature older children.

Their charm is the quiet and the ambience. They make a good escape for Mom and Dad when grandparents can mind the kids.

Azalea Plantation

This place offers four rooms for nonsmokers. It is close to the attractions of downtown and the Mid-Cities (Six Flags, Ballpark). Furnished with antiques, it may be better for older children or adults seeking a romantic getaway. There is a two-bedroom cottage with kitchen facilities that is suitable for a family wanting to be near the city but "in the country."

1400 Robinwood Drive	817-838-5882
Fort Worth, Texas 76111	800-687-3529

B&B at the Ranch

Four Western styled rooms in a country setting. Tennis court on property. Close to all attractions in Fort Worth, Mid-Cities, and Arlington. Off NE loop 820.

933 Ranch Road	817-232-5522
8275 Wagley Robertson Road	FAX: 817-232-5522
Fort Worth, Texas 76131	

Miss Molly's

As described above, a small, but classy place with unique décor.

109-1/2 West Exchange Avenue	1-800-996-6559
www.missmollys.com	

Texas White House

On the near south side in the hospital district and close to Thistle Hill, but with only three rooms so reserve ahead.

1417 Eighth Avenue	817-923-3597
Fort Worth, Texas 76104	800-279-6491
FAX: 817-923-0410	

Angel's Rest

In one of Weatherford's classic Victorian homes you'll find ten capacious rooms with private baths, king-size beds with feather mattresses on three and a half quiet landscaped acres. Call for prices and reservations for a close-to-home getaway or a nearby stop while touring the region.

1105 Palo Pinto Street	800-687-1669
P.O. Box 1571	
Weatherford, Texas 76086	

The Stagecoach Inn

On occasion, the accommodation is the destination. For a peaceful getaway, try this place south of Temple, Texas. Take I-35 to Exit 284 (take Exit 283 if you're coming from the south). Go under the Interstate and take the access road. Follow the signs. Salado is about 50 miles north of Austin and has some interesting gift and antique shopping. Once a busy stop on the Chisholm Trail, it faded when the railroads diverted traffic away from the town.

The Stagecoach Inn began as the Shady Villa Inn in the 19th century and has hosted such luminaries as Generals George Armstrong Custer and Robert E. Lee, as well as Sam Houston and Jesse James.

The grounds are restful with many large live oaks, and most of the 82 rooms have balconies or patios. But the restaurant is the reason to go there. Homestyle cookin' and plenty of it assures everyone a full belly. The fried catfish and the chicken—any way they fix it—are superb. And do not miss the pecan or lemon chess pie for dessert.

It's a great place to stop along the way to or from Austin or San Antonio. Go in the fall to hear the bagpipes when the Scots gather (Salado's founding citizens were mostly Scots of Sterling Robinson's pioneer colony).

1 Main Street　　　　　　　　254-947-5111
P.O. Box 97　　　　　　　　　1-800-732-8994
Salado, Texas 76571

Afterword

North Central Texas Council of Governments

Newcomers to the Fort Worth/Dallas area or those planning to relocate here can utilize the resources of this organization to retrieve demographics and vital statistics about the Metroplex and the surrounding sixteen-county region. The website includes economic and population statistics, crime data, information about housing starts and employment, and, best of all, *printable* aerial maps.

616 Six Flags Drive
P.O. Box 5888
Arlington, Texas 76005-5888

817-695-9150
FAX: 817-640-4428
www.dfwinfo.com

Every effort has been made to insure the accuracy of the information contained in this book. Unfortunately, we live in fast-moving times. Often, things change before the resources listing them can catch up. The telephone directory may be out-dated before it hits the porch. Businesses fail; others take their place. Addresses vary. New area codes replace old ones. Before setting out for a place mentioned in this book, call to be certain they are still there and verify hours of operation and admission charges.

Other than that, HAVE FUN, HAPPY EXPLORING!

Downtown Fort Worth. Photo courtesy of Jenny Solomon.

Index

269